Who is Grace Black? Occupational Therapy in Oregon:

Development & Historical Account of the Profession

Who is Grace Black? Occupational Therapy in Oregon
Development & Historical Account of the Profession

Sue Nelson

With Aaron Proctor & Lilian Crawford

PACIFIC UNIVERSITY LIBRARIES
FOREST GROVE, OR

Published by Pacific University Libraries 2017

Pacific University Libraries
2043 College Way
Forest Grove, Oregon 97116

© Sue Nelson, CC-BY-SA

This book is distributed under the terms of a Creative Commons Attribution-ShareAlike License, which permits commercial use, distribution, and reproduction in any medium, provided the original author and publisher are credited and any new works are licensed under identical terms.

Where noted with *, the text is an original excerpt from the 1981 book, "Reflections," authored by students and faculty of the Certified Occupational Therapy Assistant program at Mt. Hood Community College.

The author and publisher gratefully acknowledge the permission granted to reproduce the copyright material in this book.
Every effort has been made to trace copyright holders and to obtain their permission for the use of copyright material. The publisher apologizes for any errors or omissions in the above list and would be grateful if notified of any corrections that should be incorporated in future reprints or editions of this book.

Cover image: Majestic Mount Hood #62736, U.S. Department of Transportation Federal Highway Administration

ISBN 978-1-945398-96-4

BEE TREE

An imprint of the Pacific University Libraries

Our treasure lies in the beehive of our knowledge. We are perpetually on the way thither, being by nature [...] honey gathereres of the mind.

Friedrich Nietzsche

The "Bee Tree", an iconic ivy-covered tree that stood on the Pacific University campus for many years, was already old and hollow when pioneer Tabitha Brown arrived in Oregon in 1846. Mrs. Brown started a home for orphans that would grow into Pacific University. According to the Forest Grove News-Times, the tree was "said to have housed a swarm of bees who furnished the little old lady with honey which she sold to buy provisions for her orphan children."

Dedication

This book is dedicated to my Aunt Ellie (the original occupational therapist in my family) and her sister, Audrey Kerseg, my mother.

And to my husband, who has had to live with OT all of our married lives. At least I got him past the "basket-weaving" stage.

—Sue Nelson

Contents

2016 Acknowledgements	ix
Introduction from "Reflections"	xiii
Acknowledgments from "Reflections"	xv
Foreword: 2016	xvii
2016 Introduction: "Who is Grace Black?"	xxi
Biography of Grace Black	xxv
Before the Beginning: 1946	1
The Beginning: 1947-1952	9
Establishing Roots: 1953-1959	27
Certified Occupational Therapy Assistant (COTA) School: 1960-1967	45
Rehabilitation Institute of Oregon (RIO) Development: 1968-1976	73
Licensure: 1977	97
Career Mobility: 1978-1990	115
Pacific University: 1990-1999	153
The New Millennium	175

Quilts	*181*
To the Present	*217*
Before the Future	*235*
Appendices	*243*
Appendix A	*245*
Appendix B	*255*
Appendix C	*257*
Appendix D	*259*
Appendix E	*261*
Biographies of Oregon Occupational Therapists	*265*

2016 Acknowledgements

This book would not have been possible without the very generous support of my friend, John White. His deep dedication to occupational therapy and great interest in history and human accomplishments have spurred me in a writing project where I am so naïve. My own challenge comes from a love of my profession and also because I was a part of this history for so many years. And being so privileged to know those of the past who contributed so much energy and creative skills, I feel those early pioneers should not be forgotten. I want to thank all those therapists who have told their stories and submitted personal accounts for this book, so that those of you in the future may appreciate how the professional foundations are built on one another, in order to make occupational therapy in Oregon what it is today.

My partner in crime, Lilian Crawford, is responsible for much of the information up to 1980 which came from the book entitled, *Reflections*. Her major role at Mt. Hood Community College led the project that became the only known written record of that era. It was completed by the COTA students and mentored by Lilian Crawford and Sue Byers.** And I especially want to thank Molly McEwen for her wisdom and guidance in leading me towards viewing occupational therapy as a philosophy by which I live. From her I learned how deep the passion of our way of life could be and the broad meaning of diversity.

Thanks to Aaron R. Proctor, OTR/L, OTD Class of 2015 at Pacific University, who provided the technical skills to transcribe my paper and pencil efforts into exceptional results in the form of the current computer media (a foreign language for my aging brain.) Aaron also coordinated the art and photography submissions for this book. Many, many thanks, Aaron.

Lastly, and certainly most important, the "research" department of John's office, Suzie Schwab and Kelly Hering. They have been most helpful in digging into the past and the "cloud in the sky" to find information and articles that I requested. Without them I would never have known where to look. They are the detective department! Suzie has been with the OT school for 14 years and has truly gotten to know the OT profession inside and out. This is a quote from her, "OT is an amazing profession, but truly it is the people who pursue OT that are amazing. OT is so diverse in practice, and practitioners, but the common denominator is caring. It is individuals that care, care to be a part of pursing growth, not only of themselves but others. Specifically, the growth that happens when clients realize their potential, and it isn't just for a narrow population. It is reaching across ability/disability spectrum and over the life span. It is a bit mind boggling, and truly art and science wrapped up offering purpose and meaning to others lives."

And my deepest apologies to anyone I may have left out, as it would be impossible to remember everyone from the last 60 years. As the time goes on, and it looks like this book will become a reality, we salute Isaac Gilman and Johanna Meetz, of the Pacific University library, who told us it was a possibility and offered to be our publisher. This exciting venture is coming to fruition and my goal of honoring our pioneers will be professionally accomplished. Many thanks to all.

All proceeds from this book will benefit the Audrey Kerseg

Scholarship Fund within the School of Occupational Therapy at Pacific University.

—Sue Nelson

**This book has many entries from "Reflections," which are based on the accounts of the first organizations of the professional occupational therapy community.

Introduction from "Reflections"

In the Fall of each academic year, the first year occupational therapy assistant students begin their journey into the world of occupational therapy with a look at the history of the profession. They read and discuss the philosophy of Adolf Meyer and become familiar with names such as Susan Tracy, Eleanor Clarke Slagle, Helen Willard, and Clare Spackman. During this process the students always ask about the history of occupational therapy in Oregon. Fortunately they are treated to an oral history given by Jean Vann, OTR, and instructor in the O.T.A. Program. These personal accounts of the past have intrigued all of us and led to the evolution of this project. An attempt has been made to gather the history of the Occupational Therapy Association of Oregon from all of you who have been responsible for making it. Although time has blurred some of the dates and events, the spirit and essence of the association has survived. We have discovered from this experience that the "burning issues" have always been the same – Public Relations, Licensure, Recruitment, Development of an O.T.R. Program, The Role of the O.T.R. and C.O.T.A., Third Party Reimbursement –. It seems that history is like that.

Time is an important factor in change. Those who have gone before us have completed the preliminary work so that we can become agents of change – just as we are doing for those who come after us.

This continuity has given all of us a sense of identity – of belonging to an established purpose.

So join with us in experiencing REFLECTIONS – THE HISTORY OF THE OCCUPATIONAL THERAPY ASSOCIATION OF OREGON.

The Faculty and Students
O.T.A. Program
1980-81

Acknowledgments from "Reflections"

We wish to extend our appreciation to all of the therapists who have shared their memories with us. Needless to say, this project would not have been completed without their assistance.During the 1980-81 school year, Occupational Therapy Assistant (OTA) students at Mt. Hood Community College contributed hours of their time, enthusiasm, and energy. Everyone was involved in the project at one time or another. An extra special thank you is sent to the following students/graduates of the OTA program:

Chief Coordinator of Project
Sue Byers

Calligraphy
Wendy Garfield, COTA

Typists

Jenifer Eells
Lois Dahlquist
Mary McCullough
Judy Carroll
Maureen Merrill

Cheryl O'Lenic
Nanci Erickson

Graphics
InaRae Ussack, COTA

Proofreader
Virginia Poulson

Extra Assistance
Kate Phillips
Marlena Evans
Cathy Meyer
Laura Tumminia, COTA

The OTA students who worked on this project would like to make a special acknowledgement to Lilian Crawford whose effort, encouragement, endless hours, and never failing humor made this publication possible.

Foreword: 2016

Occupational therapy has been in my life since childhood. My mother was a nurse in a tuberculosis sanitarium in Wisconsin and her good friend was an occupational therapist there. When I grew up I wanted to be one of "those." And so it was!

As a graduate of the University of Minnesota in occupational therapy, I worked a few years and suddenly felt the "call of the west". My arrival in Portland in 1957 found only 18 occupational therapists in the entire state. There were also a couple in Vancouver, Washington and southern Oregon. Some were working "at home" with families, too.

There was a well-organized state association with a constitution that had been presented and approved by the National Association, AOTA, in 1947. At that time the Oregon president was Mary Boyce and the vice-president was Grace Black.

The early history of the Occupational Therapy Association of Oregon (OTAO), up to 1981, was compiled and published by the Mt. Hood Community College's Occupational Therapy Assistant program under the direction of Lilian Crawford.

Hopefully, this book will synthesize the history of occupational therapy up to 1981 and then continue on to present day. The profession grows and flourishes through social changes, advancing medical challenges, and the creativity of young ideas and energies that build upon past experiences of those who came before us.

We have tried to gather documents and personal narratives from currently known resources and from many places in tucked away corners. The first is in the book, *Reflections: The History of the Occupational Therapy Association of Oregon*.

The second place we found more records is in Jean Vann's attic; where we were told there are innumerable boxes stacked up not quite in chronological order. And these boxes have piled up since the beginning.

The third place is a recently described "lock box" in Hillsboro, Oregon, where there is a secret location no one seems to know about. In that treasury are OTAO membership directories, copies of the OTAO membership newsletters, "The Viewpoint" (newsletter), and annual reports.

And the fourth place is in our hearts and memories.

This book is not intended to be a documentary. Please think of it as a chronological conversation – reconnecting with therapists of the past – those who have made our profession what it is today. Each and every one has contributed their time and their space to the richness of occupational therapy. Our profession brings together many persons who value service to others and who seek to find those skills that bring quality of life to a world that is very diverse. It is our goal to bring some balance to living and to problem solve the many things that may confront us throughout our lives and our practice. And to let those in the future, meet the real people that are the foundation of our OT in Oregon. Our stories build upon each other and strengthen the foundation, which presents the quality and diversity of today's occupational therapy philosophy. Furthermore, it is deliberately celebrating the historical context and contributions of past practitioners. Emerging practitioners will also benefit from these stories to support current practice by honoring OTAO's roots.

This text can also be thought of as an attempt to electronically record and organize historical OTAO documents so that future generations may understand the many challenges and triumphs of the last 70 years.

Readers will find a variety of images woven within the following chapters. Images were chosen from current and past occupational therapy students at Pacific University who were asked to contribute "iconic Oregon images" as a way to represent the impeccable beauty our great state of Oregon has to offer.

Robert Bing, in his forward to Occupational Therapy: The First 30 Years by Virginia A.M. Quiroga, stated, "Reading our history should be of particular value to a younger generation of shakers and movers who fervently believe that their world is new, that all their problems are freshly minted, and that they need only employ reason and emotion to come to some resolution."

—Sue Nelson

2016 Introduction: "Who is Grace Black?"

I decided to name the title of this text after Grace Black, a very successful and influential occupational therapist. I have heard the name of Grace Black since coming to Oregon many years ago. Her name and memories of her accomplishments have inspired many through history. She represents the creative energy of a true pioneer – making something out of very little. She gathered the first groups of therapists together to form the state association that we know of today as OTAO. A constitution was drafted under Grace Black's direction (see Appendices) and presented to the American Occupational Therapy Association. When it was approved, the Occupational Therapy Association of Oregon was born.

A while back, one of the faculty members at Pacific's University School of Occupational Therapy was honored with the Grace Black Award. John White, program director, asked me who Grace Black was and if I knew her. This experience helped me realize that Grace Black's legacy has been largely unrecognized. I decided at that moment her story must be heard.

In 1957 when I moved "out west" I stayed with my uncle Glen, a pediatrician in Vancouver, Washington. He took me to visit Oregon Health & Science University (OHSU) in Portland, Oregon.

(Back then it was called "The County Hospital" or "TB Hospital". It was here that he introduced me to an occupational therapist named, Grace Black. I also visited the Rehabilitation Institute of Oregon (RIO) and met another occupational therapist, Clara Brainard and the medical director, Dr. Ray Moore. Ruth Ann Moore, Dr. Moore's wife, is also an occupational therapist that had worked with Grace Black.

In order to write some kind of article about Ms. Black, I went to see Jean Vann, an occupational therapists that was close to retirement. She had the paper history of OTAO filed in many boxes in her attic. When I got to Jean's, the dining room table was covered with files and papers. I was madly taking notes when Jean said, "Did you know that Grace was laid to rest over at Willamette Cemetery and Mausoleum? She has an urn there." Jean called to find out if the cemetery was open and discovered they would be open for only 45 minutes longer so we hopped into her car with cameras in hand so we could take pictures of Grace's plaque.

Willamette Cemetery is a very large building with three floors and many levels of chambers. The downstairs chambers are very dark and the light switches were difficult to find. Although we had a map and the location, it was challenging to find our way. Our search took us through many chambers until we finally found Grace's plaque. Jean, who is always prepared, had a pen light in her purse and shined it up on the plaque while I stood on my tiptoes and took a photo. When we turned to leave it was even harder to retrace our steps. We finally found our way to the exit gate but it wouldn't open because it was after closing time. There we were... locked in the mausoleum! When we finally calmed down, Jean realized she had her cell phone and she called her husband to tell him about our dilemma. He phoned the office to find some heavenly person who let us out.

Wonderful stories like these are the weft of our profession. Because of who we are, we learn from the lessons of the past, treasure the connections of those that precede us, and weave the past together with the future.

Join us on this historical journey as we share our stories, celebrate the life of Grace Black, and honor the historical roots of OTAO.

—Sue Nelson

Biography of Grace Black

Grace Black, R.N., OTR
Born: 1906; Died: 1967

© Aaron R. Proctor, OTD, OTR/L, Pacific University Class of 2015. Used with Permission

Grace Black graduated in 1930 from Western Reserve University in Cleveland, Ohio as a nurse. She practiced as a nurse and then pursued an occupational therapy degree at Columbian University. Her OT career began in Detroit, Michigan at the Curative Workshop 1945-46.

Grace is described as a plain looking blonde person of medium height who moved to Portland in 1947, and developed the first OT position at what was then called "the county hospital", the "TB Hospital", the Medical School Hospital and now Oregon Health & Science University (OHSU). She lived on Hamilton Street, "up on the hill."

It was there that I met Grace Black when my uncle, a physician, brought me "up to the hill" (trying to recruit me to move out from Michigan) to introduce me to this remarkable lady. After our meeting, he took me to lunch at the Hillvilla Restaurant (now the Chart House) overlooking beautiful Portland and the Willamette River on a gorgeous sunny day. That was in 1957!

Grace Black had OT students who came from all over for fieldwork training. She loved her students and she put all her energy into occupational therapy.

There was no insurance payments for services and no departmental budget. In order to buy supplies, if a patient did a craft, they had to make two of them. One was put in a display case to sell. The display case was open all the time and a volunteer was on duty to sell the items. This became her operating budget. Grace had some patients that she taught hardanger (a form of whitework embroidery.) And she could do anything with an empty cardboard toilet paper roll. She was very well liked by her patients.

Grace was active in organizing the local occupational therapists and wrote the first constitution for OTAO in 1947. She became the first vice president and the president in 1950-51.

Grace had a bad heart as a result of having mumps as a child. She died during her lunch hour in the hospital cafeteria. A service was held for her at Portland Memorial and she is interned at Willamette Cemetery and Mausoleum (renamed: Wilhelm Portland Memorial Funeral Home and Mausoleum).

Much of this information came from Jean Vann during an interview in 2013 as we have tried to document the early history of occupational therapy in Oregon.

—Sue Nelson

1
Before the Beginning: 1946

Opal Creek (near Lyons, Oregon). © Aaron R. Proctor, OTD, OTR/L, Pacific University Class of 2015. Used with Permission.

"I have always enjoyed capturing the pure beauty of Oregon in pencil sketches and photography. Living in this gorgeous part of our country is something I am consistently grateful for. Connecting with nature makes me feel peaceful and alive."
—Aaron R. Proctor

Multnomah Falls. © Martha Wegner, OTD, OTR/L, Pacific University Class of 2015. Used with permission.

"Photography has played a significant role in my life since I was a young child learning how to shoot photos with my father in the northern Minnesota wilderness areas. I continue to find enjoyment capturing the stillness, beauty, and joyful expression of nature in all landscapes I visit."
—Martha Wegner

Formation of the American Occupational Association (AOTA)

On March 15, 1917, the American Occupational Therapy Association (AOTA) was founded in Clifton Springs, New York. The six original signers were George Edward Barton, Thomas B. Kidner, the Misses Isabel G. Newton and Susan C. Johnson, Mrs. Eleanor Clarke Slagle and Dr. William Rush Dunton.

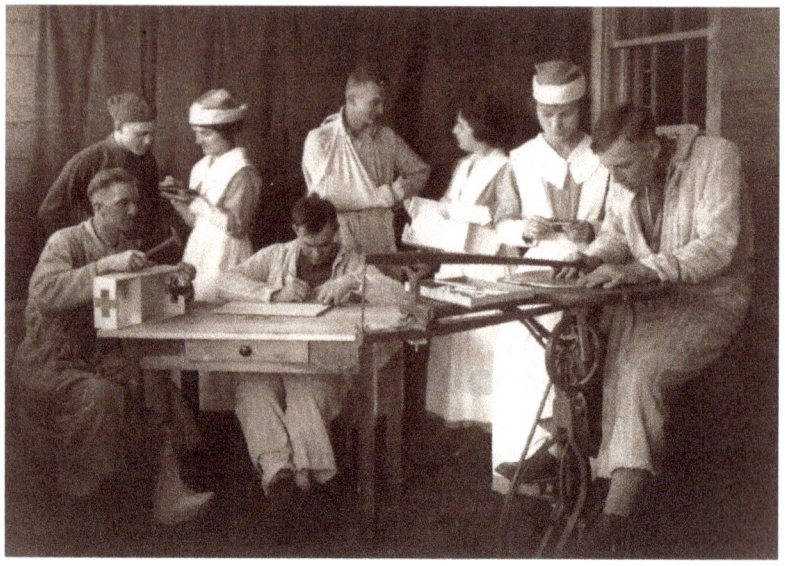

Reconstruction aides supervise recovering servicemen in craft activities in the early years of World War I. © AOTA, 1992 calendar. Used with permission.

In that year of 1917 the practicing of the unknown field of occupational therapy was in the minds and perceptions of only a few farsighted physicians. It is interesting to note that these physicians were by and large psychiatrists.

Occupational therapy provides services to individuals whose ability to cope with the tasks of living are threatened or impaired by developmental deficiencies, the aging process, physical injury or illness, or psychological disability. Early founders of the profession deemed it necessary to develop an organization that could help advocate for growth and development of occupational therapy practice worldwide (Gordon, 2009).

Gordon, D. M. (2009). The history of occupational therapy. In E. B. Crepeau, E. S. Cohn & B. A. B. Schell (Eds.), *Willard & Spackman's occupational therapy* (11th ed., pp. 202-215). Philadelphia, PA: Lippincott.

Association pioneers Helen Willard and Sidney Bottner at the E.D. Hines, Jr. Hospital, Maywood, Illinois, 1924. © AOTA, 1992 calendar. Used with permission.

"This V.A. facility is where I had my physical disabilities fieldwork experience in 1953. Most of the patients had been injured in the Korean War. Some of them were blind and many had serious skin conditions."
—Sue Nelson

Formation of the Occupational Therapy Association of Oregon (OTAO), 1946

Within Oregon, occupational therapists were first seen in the federal veteran affairs hospitals soon after the end of World War II. Within the state hospitals, occupational therapy was recognized as a need and departments began forming at the University of Oregon Medical School, Hospital for Crippled Children, and Salem State Hospital. Programs at the Rehabilitation Institute of Oregon, Holliday Park Hospital and many others also started during this time.

The Occupational Therapy Association of Oregon began in 1946 with less than 20 members. In the winter of 1946, at a meeting of the Washington Occupational Therapy Association, the question arose as to the advisability of organizing an Occupational Therapy Association in the state of Oregon. The question arose because of two factors. One, with an increase in the number of registered therapists in Oregon, it was now feasible. Two, geographically, it was more practical to have an organization in Oregon so that more of the therapists could attend meetings. Also, it was felt that the addition of another state association on the west coast would strengthen the position of those western delegates already [had] members of the National House of Delegates.

During the following months, several informal meetings of interested therapists were held to discuss the problems of organization and appoint a committee to draft a constitution. The constitution was drafted by a committee of four [people] with Grace Black as chairman.

During this period of organization, the occupational therapists on the staff at the Veterans Hospital in Vancouver, Washington, were active participants in all planning. Their membership in the Oregon Association was mutually desirable, both because of their geographic location and the fact of their administrative supervision by the Portland Veterans Hospital.

The first draft of the constitution was submitted to the group by the constitution committee on March 8, 1947. The final draft was submitted to Edna Ellen Bell, [on] June 11, 1947, for presentation to the National Association.

Submitted for the permanent record
By Shirley Bowing, Secretary,
August 1947 to February 1949

Information obtained from early participants in formation of state association.

2
The Beginning: 1947-1952

© Daniel Tautenhan, LMT, MBA, OTD, Pacific University Class of 2017. Used with permission.

"An artist at heart, I have always been inspired by the creativity found in healing practices. My creative interests have led me to explore a wide variety of edifying occupations and roles; to evolve, and to find meaningful pathways for discovery and service. I find restorative peace through the expression of art, yoga, engaging with nature, and by my relationship with horses." —Daniel Tautenhan

An early logo of the Occupational Therapy Association of Oregon (left) and a later logo (right). © OTAO. Used with permission.

Occupational Therapy Association of Oregon*

August 14, 1947

This meeting was planned for the purpose of electing officers and determining certain policies of the organization. The meeting was called to order by the Temporary Chairman, Miss Mary Boyce. At the request of the chairman, Miss Grace A. Black acted as recording secretary of the meeting.

The roll call was as follows:

Miss Betty Coulter, Roseburg Veterans Hospital
Miss Helen Taragos, Veterans Administration, Portland
Miss Mary Boyce, Veterans Administration, Portland
Miss Marjorie Englehart, Veterans Administration, Portland
Mrs. Ruth Ann Moore, Veterans Administration, Portland
Mrs. Eloise Irwin, Portland
Miss Martha Mae Lasche, Morningside Hospital, Portland
Miss Grace A. Black, University of Oregon Medical School, Portland

Guests [who] were present at the meeting were:

Miss Edna Ellen Bell, Director of Occupational Therapy and Rehabilitation, College of Puget Sound, Tacoma, Washington
Miss Jeanette Blake, student from College of Puget Sound
Miss Eileen Boyd, student from College of Puget Sound

Those individuals who were considered to be interested in membership but who were not present were listed as follows:

Miss Lydia Waller
Miss Shirley Bowing
Mrs. Evelyn Brill
Miss Carol Haskins
Mrs. Dorothy Jeusin
Miss Joy Eftelin
Mrs. Anne Kronenberg
Mrs. Julia Strode
Miss Lucille Parker

The elections and results of voting for officers was as follows:

President: Miss Mary Boyce, Unanimously elected

Vice President: Miss Grace A. Black, Unanimously elected

Secretary: Miss Shirley Bowing, Unanimously elected

Treasurer: Miss Helen Taragos, Unanimously elected

Delegate: Miss Marjorie Englehart, Four votes

Alternate Delegate: Miss Martha Mae Lasche, Three votes

Representative elected from the body to serve on the Board of Managers:

Mrs. Ruth Anne Moore

The election of Delegate and Alternate Delegate was determined from the three nominees: Miss Marjorie Englehart, Miss Martha Mae Lasche, and Mrs. Ruth Anne Moore by the largest vote return indicating the Delegate, the second largest vote to indicate the alternate. Obligations and duties of the Delegate were explained to the group by request.

The discussion concerning dues followed election of officers. The needs of the organization were determined to be primarily the contribution to the expenses of the delegate to the convention the first week in November. Motion was made and seconded that the dues for the Occupational Therapy Association of Oregon should be three [dollars] ($3.00) a year, payable at the September meeting.

It was suggested that a new by-law should be incorporated in the Constitution whereby the reciprocity with other state associations should be made clear for collection dues from transferring members. It was suggested that this question be held until the Delegate should have the opportunity of hearing this question discussed at the meetings in November, (House of Delegates) as Miss Bell informed the group that this question is under discussion by other state associations.

A letter addressed to Miss Martha Mae Lasche from Miss Marian Davis, OTR, President of the Occupational Therapy Association of Southern California, was read by the President to the membership. This letter requested the organization to consider membership in the Association of Western Hospitals. Miss Lasche's letter in answer to this request was read to the membership and their wishes requested.

It was considered advisable to investigate the Association of Western Hospitals before any definite decisions were made. The Secretary, Association of Western Hospitals, 870 Market Street, San Francisco, California, for information. One question which should be answered is regarding dues in this association. Does the five dollar ($5.00) dues come from the association as a whole or is each member expected to pay this fee?

Miss Bell offered to see that the question of membership in the Washington Association of those (now) members of the Occupational Therapy Association of Oregon was cleared and any dues paid to the Occupational Therapy Association of Washington be transferred to this Treasurer.

It was moved and seconded that the next meeting be held the last Friday in September.

Discussion of those individuals and organizations that should be approached regarding Associate Membership resulted in a list of those to whom letters should be addressed accordingly by the Secretary. This list is attached to the minutes. Dues for Associate Members was moved and seconded to be two dollars ($2.00), dues for students to be none.

It was moved and seconded that the meeting adjourn. The meeting was held from 7:30pm to 9pm.

OTAO Executive Board Members

1947*

President: Mary Boyce

Vice President: Grace Black

Secretary: Shirley Bowing

Treasurer: Betty Coulter

Delegate: Dorothy Ross

Alternative Delegate: Carol Haskins

Potential Membership of

The Occupational Therapy Association of Oregon

August 14, 1947

O. T.	Address
Black, Miss Grace A.	University of Oregon Medical School
Bowing, Miss Shirley	Barnes Hospital, Vancouver, Washington
Boyce, Miss Mary	Veterans Administration, Portland, Oregon
Brill, Mrs. Evelyn	Barnes Hospital, Vancouver, Washington
Coulter, Miss Betty	Veterans Administration, Roseburg, Oregon
Eftelin, Miss Joy	Barnes Hospital, Vancouver, Washington
Englemart, Miss Marjorie	Veterans Administration, Portland, Oregon
Haskins, Miss Carol	Hahnemann Hospital
Irwin, Mrs. Eloise	
Jenkins, Mrs. Dorothy	
Kronenberg, Mrs. Anne	

O. T. (Continued)	Address
Lasche, Miss Martha Mae	Morningside Hospital
Moore, Mrs. Ruth Ann	Veterans Administration, Portland, Oregon
Parker, Miss Lucille	
Strode, Mrs. Julia	
Taragos, Miss Helen	Veterans Administration, Portland, Oregon
Waller, Miss Lydia	Barnes Hospital, Vancouver, Washington

OCCUPATIONAL THERAPY ASSOCIATION OF OREGON

GENERAL MEETING: Nov. 21, 1947

The meeting was held in the library building at the University of Oregon Medical School and was called to order by the president, Mary Boyce.

The minutes of the previous meeting were read and approved.

The guest speaker, Captain Wynn of the U.S. Army recruiting office, reported on the Women's Medical Auxillary Corp.

Margaret Englehart and Carol Haskins reported on the annual AOTA meeting which they had attended in California. They reported that the constitution of the Oregon Occupational Therapy Association had been approved with one minor correction (Article 2-Section 2).

The treasurer's report was read and approved (Cash on hand: $21.00)

A letter from Southern California OT Association was read and raised the question of a contribution by the Oregon Association towards the expense of the National Convention.

A motion was made to give a $5 donation. This was voted down.

A motion was made and approved that a donation be raised through a special assessment of $1 per member.

A motion was made and approved that Carol Haskins be appointed as program-chairman for a special meeting in February.

A motion was made and approved that the meeting be adjourned.

Respectfully submitted,
Shirley M. Bowing, Secretary

The below excerpt is included to demonstrate how states chose to work together for common causes. It was crucial during the early years of OTAO to expand knowledge and efforts of the organization in hopes to increase membership.

WESTERN INTERNATIONAL CONFERENCE OF OCCUPATIONAL & PHYSICAL THERAPY

The Western International Conference of Occupational and Physical Therapy was formed in 1949. At first the meetings alternated between the United States and Canada, and the United States meetings between Washington and Oregon. They soon alternated between each of the three participants. Each state or province would alternate having the president of one association as chairman and the president of the other association as vice-chairman. Until about 1964, the treasury travelled to each participating area. At that time, funds were held up, and each area developed and held its own treasury.

A theme was chosen for each meeting and local speakers were asked to participate. Many excellent physicians spoke to the group. Participation at the meetings ranged from 100 to probably 300. A luncheon speaker and banquet speaker were usually included in the program.

The meeting was generally an all-day Saturday meeting with a planning breakfast for the presidents of each area to plan for the next year's meeting.

The need in the beginning was for information and support of the therapists ion the Northwest; Oregon, Washington, and British Columbia. Most departments were single person departments. Each person needed the others. As the numbers of therapists grew in each area, the need for WIC (Western International Conference) OT-PT decreased until about 1966 in Vancouver, British Columbia when only two occupational therapists and two physical therapists from Oregon attended. The Vancouver therapists had to guarantee hotel rooms and pay for them, even if not occupied, if they had held them. Thanks to therapists coming from the rest of Canada, they managed to stay in the black. The treasuries were divided among the state or province associations.

Some of the benefits of WIC OT-PT were a closer working association with occupational therapy and physical therapy in Oregon. A knowledge of what therapists and therapy departments were accomplishing in Washington and British Columbia was invaluable. This organization served a very good purpose.

—Jean Vann

1948*

President: Mary Boyce

Vice President: Grace Black

Secretary: Shirley Bowing

Treasurer: Betty Coulter

Delegate: Dorothy Ross

Alternative Delegate: Carol Haskins

Major Events:

1. The major concerns for this year revolved around the growth and development of the association as well as becoming involved in national issues.

OCCUPATIONAL THERAPY ASSOCIATION OF OREGON*

GENERAL MEETING – October 29, 1948

The meeting was held at the home of Ruth Ann Moore and was called to order by the president, Mary Boyce.

The minutes of the previous meeting were read and approved.

The president appointed the following members as nominating committee for the coming election of officers:

Grace Black, Chairman
Dorothy Ross
Mary Kiosse

Carol Haskins, alternate delegate, gave a detailed report on the annual American Occupational Therapy Association convention in New York, where she represented the Occupational Therapy Association of Oregon.

The motion was made and approved that the therapists in Idaho and Montana be invitied to attend meetings.

An informal discussion centered around the possibility of the Oregon association stimulating interest in the employment of registered occupational therapists for the state hospitals. The suggestion that Miss Boyce and Miss Black spearhead this movement by contacting Miss Joslyn met with the memberships approval.

The motion was made and approved that the meeting adjourn.

Respectfully submitted,
Shirley M. Bowing, Secretary

1949*

President: Mary Boyce

Vice President: Betty Warren

Secretary: Dorothy Seidehamel

Treasurer: Betty Coulter

Delegate: Carol Haskins

Alternative Delegate: Mary Kiosse

Major Events:

1. Fourteen occupational therapists were members of OTAO.

2. The priority issue for the year was recruitment of students for occupational therapy schools.

3. The annual meeting of the American Occupational Therapy Association was held in Detroit, Michigan.

4. There were seven occupational therapy departments in Oregon including Eugene Spastic Clinic, Portland Rehabilitation Center, University of Oregon Medical School, Morningside, Portland V. A., Vancouver V. A., and Roseburg V. A.

5. OTAO joined Washington and California as a section in the Association of Western Hospitals.

6. The following is a quote from Caroline Haskins, OTAO Delegate: "It is not what the patient does to the material, but what the material does for the patient that is important."

7. May 6, 1949 was the first state wide meeting held at the Portland Rehabilitation Center. The purpose of the meeting was to publicize the profession.

1950*

President: Grace Black

Vice President: Hope Lee

Secretary: Janet Ranyard

Treasurer: Ann Kehm

Delegate/Alternative Delegate: Mary Kiosse/Josephine Kind

Major Events:

1. At the December membership meeting, each member was asked to procure and dress a doll to be given to the Toy and Joy Program.

2. The sum of one hundred dollars ($100.00) was used from the treasury to send the delegate to the national conference which was held in Colorado Springs, Colorado.

3. Association fund raising projects included:

    a) Sale of matches with the state seal them.

    b) Sale of personalized return address seals.

    c) Sale of social calendars "Social Capers", ($1.00 each)

4. Jean Nystrom (Vann), Betty Irle, and Evelyn Brill were new members. Occupational therapists spoke at a career day [event] at Milwaukie High School

6. Grace Black offered (for a nominal fee) to obtain condensed versions of Robert's Rules of Order for any OTAO member who wished them. Radio Station KPOJ was contacted to make sure that occupational therapy was included in their "Careers Unlimited" program.

8. Wilma West, OTR is director (executive) of the American Occupational Therapy Association. Winifred C. Kahmann, OTR, is the president. The Second Conference of Occupational and Physical Therapists (western section) was held in Seattle, Washington, April 22 -23, 1950. The theme of the conference was "Education."

1951*

President: Grace Black

Vice President: Barbara Viesko

Secretary: Jean Vann

Treasurer: Amy Uchimoto

Delegate: Elizabeth Coulter

Alternative Delegate: Janet Ranyard

*Elizabeth went into the Army and Janet became delegate

Major Events:

1. A suggested money making project for the association was to sponsor a Blue Room night at the Civic Theater.

2. The April membership meeting included a going away party for Shirley Bowing (she was leaving to become director of the OT program at the College of Puget Sound.)

3. At Your Fingertips booklet available from AOTA for $2.00

4. Other Fund Raisers: Social Capers (date books) – each member was to sell six (6) books. The OT Department at the Vancouver V. A. raffled off a water color painting and donate the $24.00 to OTAO.

5. The Annual Meeting was held March 23, 1951, at the Portland Rehabilitation Center.

6. The Western International Conference of Occupational and Physical Therapy was held in Canada. The them was – "Geriatrics and Problems of the Crippled Child"

1952*

President: Jean Vann

Vice President: Evelyn Brill

Secretary: Mary Minglin

Treasurer: Clara Brainard

Delegate: Jan Ranyard

Alternative Delegate: Fran Heermans

Major Events:

1. This is the first year that the association has monthly meetings. They are the first Friday of every month except July and August at 7:30pm.

2. OTAO membership dues are three dollars ($3.00).

3. The membership discussed the issue of licensure at the November meeting.

4. The Fourth Western International Conference of Occupational and Physical Therapists was held at the Multnomah Hotel in Portland (May 31 – June 1, 1952). The theme of the conference was – "Search and Research". Grace Black was chairman of the conference.

6. OTAO had display at the Multnomah Hotel for the Oregon Tuberculosis and Health Association Conference.

7. Meier and Frank was contacted regarding the use of their windows for a publicity display for occupational therapy.

3
Establishing Roots: 1953-1959

This patch will be familiar to many occupational therapists. It was typically attached, sewn, or ironed on white hospital uniforms worn during World War II. The patch helped inform patients and colleagues of our unique health care skills and, no doubt, sparked the familiar question, "What exactly is occupational therapy?" Patch provided by OTAO.

The below information is included so readers may understand how OTs recruited new people to the profession. Recruitment material was commonly sent to prospective OTs by AOTA and OTAO.

MODEL TALK ON OCCUPATIONAL THERAPY*

Time: About 6 minutes

A CAREER OF SERVICE IN OCCUPATIONAL THERAPY

1951

It is recommended that the professional therapist making this talk be accompanied by a student, wearing the uniform of her [their] school.

WHAT IS OCCUPATIONAL THERAPY?

It is a form of treatment in which handcrafts, recreation and creative work in the arts are used, either to produce favorable emotional responses or to overcome physical disabilities through exercise of the injured part.

Many people think of occupational therapy as making things, such as baskets or leather pocketbooks. It is true that handcrafts are very useful in occupational therapy because they appeal to nearly everyone, but many other activities are also used as treatment. Study courses, painting, dramatic arts, music, games and social events may all have a part in the occupational therapy program.

The occupational therapist is trained to administer and adapt these activities to aid the recovery of the sick or disabled. This is done according to a prescription given by the patient's doctor or psychiatrist. In each case, the patient's capacity, as well as his [their] state of mind, will determine the way in which occupational therapy will be applied. The therapist keeps records and advises the doctor of the patient's progress under the treatment.

FIELDS OF OCCUPATIONAL THERAPY

In the mental hospitals, an occupational therapist will work with patients who have lost contact with reality. Painting, clay modeling, and recreational activities, as well as handicrafts provide valuable outlets for deep feelings of inferiority and anxiety.

With physical disabilities, occupational therapy uses handcrafts for active exercise to supplement physical therapy, which employs heat, light, massage, etc.

The occupational therapist is the child's friend. It is she who supplies him with bright yarns, crayons, paints, and diverting toys. A child may be exercising his paralyzed legs while riding a tricycle, or improving finger coordination while pulling colored pegs from a peg board.

With tuberculosis, occupational therapy keeps the patient cheerful, relieving his anxiety, and diverting his mind. It also has a part in vocational re-education, which is important in full rehabilitation.

(If time permits, tell human interest stories illustrative of each of the above fields.)

OCCUPATIONAL THERAPY IS A PROFESSION FOR BOTH MEN AND WOMEN

To qualify for the title, OCCUPATIONAL THERAPISTS, REGISTERD (OTR), one must go to a school of occupational therapy accredited by the AMERICAN MEDICAL ASSOCIATION.

Students are graduated with: BS in Occupational Therapy or Degree of the College, plus Occupational Therapy certificate. (Use whichever statements apply.)

If you already have a bachelor's degree, you can attend an Occupational Therapy school for 16 months and earn a certificate in Occupational Therapy. Only men and women with a degree, or a certificate in occupational therapy, are eligible to take the Occupational Therapy Registration examination, conducted twice a year by the AMERICAN OCCUPATIONAL THERAPY ASSOCIATION.

WHAT KINDS OF JOBS AFTER GRADUATION?

Qualified men and women occupational therapists are in great demand by the Veteran's Administration, state hospitals for the mentally ill and municipal, private and voluntary hospitals. Curative work-shops, rehabilitation institutes and the like are increasing in number, and would probably be even more numerous if sufficient personnel could be found to staff them.

WHAT ABOUT SALARIES?

Salary scales have improved since the war, but vary, depending on location, size of institution and responsibilities assumed. Generally, tax-supported institutions pay higher salaries. Moreover, workers are under Civil Service, and therefore enjoy job security and liberal vacation and sick-leave allowances as well as attractive pension rights. The workweek is usually 40 – 44 hours. The Veteran's Administration offers $3,100 to the beginning Registered Occupational Therapist, OTR, which is about tops for first jobs. Promotion and salary increases will depend on experience and ability to handle responsibility. Ability to pass competitive promotional examination is often required. After a few years' experience, salaries of $4,300 are not unusual. Top executives may earn up to $7,000.

THE ARMED FORCES

The U.S. Army and Air Force commission qualified occupational therapists, as 2nd Lieutenants or better, depending on age, educational background and experience. Salary in this grade is from $2,592 to $3,384. The last figure includes allowances for dependents, if any.

COULD I MAKE GOOD AS AN OCCUPATIONAL THERAPIST?

Occupational Therapy is a field rich in variety and human satisfactions. There is a big job to be done in it, and for many years there will be opportunities for many kinds of talent and ability. Are you at your best working with people? Do you like work which challenges your ingenuity and resourcefulness? Are you looking for a profession that combines interesting and varied activities with helping others? Have you a knack for handwork, combined with a scientific bent which inclines you to a career in the medical arts? Boys and girls who answer YES to these questions will find occupational therapy a deeply satisfying lifework. (Emphasize opportunities for male therapists.)

Reference might be made to the following:

"Rehabilitation Team Needs New Members," Occupational Trends, V. 2 No. 1,

Sept.-Oct. 1950.

"Careers for Tomorrow," The American Observer, Oct. 16, 1950.

"Planning Your Career," The Weekly News Review, Oct. 9, 1950.

Sketch and Photo of Anne Nicholson, OTR, Glamour, Sept. 1950.

The Occupational Outlook Handbook Bul. 940, U.S. Dept. of Labor, Ref. D.O.T. 0-32.04.

*Recruitment material sent by A.O.T.A. to each state association.

Mobile carts bearing the OT insignia carried therapeutic activities to the bedside in a World War II military hospital. © AOTA, 1992 calendar. Used with permission.

The following list of OT Programs provides a glimpse into how far our profession has come from a national perspective. According to AOTA, there are now 14 accredited doctoral (OTD) programs, 167 accredited master (MOT) programs, and 229 accredited certified OT assistant programs.

OCCUPATIONAL THERAPY SCHOOLS*

(1952/1953)

The following are the schools which have been approved by the Council on Medical Education and Hospitals of the American Medical Association:

BOSTON SCHOOL OF OCCUPATIONAL THERAPY, in affiliation with Tufts College – Boston, Massachusetts

COLUMBIA UNIVERSITY – New York, New York

UNIVERSITY OF ILLINOIS – Chicago, Illinois

THE STATE UNIVERSITY OF IOWA – Iowa City, Iowa

KALAMAZOO SCHOOL OF OCCUPATIONAL THERAPY – Western Michigan College of Education – Kalamazoo, Michigan

UNIVERSITY OF KANSAS – Lawrence, Kansas

MICHIGAN STATE NORMAL COLLEGE – Ypsilanti, Michigan

MILLS COLLEGE – Oakland, California

MILWAUKEE DOWNER COLLEGE – Milwaukee, Wisconsin

UNIVERSITY OF MINNESOTA – Minneapolis, Minnesota

MOUNT MARY COLLEGE – Milwaukee, Wisconsin

UNIVERSITY OF NEW HAMPSHIRE – Durham, New Hampshire

NEW YORK UNIVERSITY – New York, New York

OHIO STATE UNIVERSITY – Columbus, Ohio

PHILADELPHIA SCHOOL OF OCCUPATIONAL THERAPY, affiliated with the University of Pennsylvania – Philadelphia, Pennsylvania

COLLEGE OF PUGET SOUND – Tacoma, Washington

RICHMOND PROFESSIONAL INSTITUTE of the College of William and Mary – Richmond, Virginia

COLLEGE OF ST. CATHERINE – St. Paul, Minnesota

SAN JOSE STATE COLLEGE – San Jose, California

UNIVERSITY OF SOUTHERN CALIFORNIA – Los Angeles, California

TEXAS STATE COLLEGE FOR WOMEN – Denton, Texas

UNIVERSITY OF TORONTO – Toronto, Canada

1953*

President: Jean Vann

Vice President: Betty Irle & Judy Lippold (after June)

Secretary: Louise Weidlich & Joyce Wong (after September)

Treasurer: Clara Brainard Smithhisler

Delegate: Barbara Vieske & Grace Black (after June)

Alternative Delegate: Grace Black & Flora Fisher (after June)

Major Events:

1. There were 18 occupational therapists in Oregon this year:

Miss Mary Ann Best
Ruthann Betlach
Miss Mary Boyce
Miss Grace Black
Miss Clara Brainard
Mrs. Evelyn Brill
Miss Jean Dion
Miss Audrey Dooley
Miss Virginia Hatch
Mrs. Charlotte Howland
Miss Nancy Hulings
Miss Betty Irle
Mr. Robert Miller
Miss Mary Minglin
Mrs. Jean Vann
Mrs. Louise Weidlich
Miss Helen Wood
Mrs. Martha Mitchell

2. Three new facilities were developed during this year. They included: Sacred Heart Hospital, Eugene; Matson Memorial Hospital, Milwaukie; and Good Samaritan, Portland.

3. The 36th Annual Conference of the American Occupational Therapy Association was held in Houston, Texas on November 13-20, 1953.

4. The Fifth Annual Western International Conference of Occupational and Physical Therapists was held in Vancouver, B.C., on May 30-31, 1953. The theme of the conference was "Progress Together".

5. At the general membership meeting in November, there was a general discussion on the issue of licensure. No action was taken by the group at this time.

6. Grace Black developed a membership roster as a personal project.

7. OTAO contacted the Physical Therapy and Nursing Associations to learn how to find out about bills that were pertinent to our association in the State Legislature.

8. Fund Raising project suggested by Clara Brainard Smithhisler: Sell raffle tickets on a large doll that the therapists have made a layette for. The tickets were to sell for twenty-five cents each and each therapist was to sell forty tickets. The "Baby Doll" was raffled off in December and won by a volunteer at the Portland Rehabilitation Center who had a five year old girl.

1954*

President: Louise Weidlich

Vice President: Betty Irle

Secretary: Robert Miller

Treasurer: Mary Ann Best

Delegate: Grace Black

Alternative Delegate: Mary Boyce

Major Events:

1. There were eighteen working Occupational Therapists and seven "at home" therapists in 1954.

2. Occupational Therapy Departments at this time included:

Holladay Park Hospital – 1 therapist

Morningside Hospital – 2 therapists

Portland Rehabilitation Center – 2 therapists

University of Oregon Medical School – 2 therapists

V.A. Hospital – Portland – 3 therapists

V.A. Hospital – Vancouver – 3 therapists

Oregon State Hospital – 1 therapist

Children's Hospital School – 2 therapists

V.A. Hospital – Roseburg – 2 therapists

3. The following motion was made at the March 5, 1954 membership meeting: Grace Black made a motion that was

in answer to a letter from the national office, that we indicate an interest in, and recognition of the need for, or comparable status for, non-professional personnel, for OT aides and/or assistants. It was seconded by Mary Boyce and approved.

1955*

President: Louise Weidlich

Vice President: Jean Vann

Secretary: Robert Miller

Treasurer: Fredda Lamp

Delegate: Grace Black

Alternative Delegate: Mary Boyce

Major Events:

1. The focus again this year is on recruitment.

2. The 7th annual Western International Conference of Occupational and Physical Therapy was held in British Columbia.

1956*

President: Elizabeth Irle

Vice President: Robert Glass

Secretary: Ann Thompson

Treasurer: Marilyn Forse

Delegate: Evelyn Bengson

Alternative Delegate: Louise Weidlich

Major Events:

1. OTAO is the largest that it has ever been with twenty five active members and five associate members. The aim of the association during this year is to make the meetings as constructive as possible. Jan Beelan, OTR, starts the occupational therapy department at Holladay Center.

2. The 8th Annual Western International Conference of Occupational and Physical Therapists is held in Portland at the Masonic Temple (May 19 and 20). The theme for the conference is "Pain". Articles on occupational therapy appear in RN (nursing journal and McCalls Needlework.)

4. A Rehabilitation Institute was offered by the University of Oregon in cooperation with the Oregon Division of Vocational Rehabilitation and Oregon Tuberculosis and Health Association (July 29 – August 10, 1956). The purpose of the institute was to provide a basic training to representatives from the various communities that will lead to better integration and teamwork in serving the handicapped throughout the state.

5. Fund Raising Projects included:

1. Non working occupational therapists sponsored a cookie and cookie dough sale at the monthly meetings; Christmas card sale; A complete layette was designed and made for a doll that was raffled off at the December meeting.

1957*

President: Robert Glass

Vice President: Elizabeth Callahan

Secretary: Margaret Drake

Treasurer: Dorothy Richards

Delegate: Evelyn Bengson

Alternative Delegate: Ruth Pray

Major Events:

1. Governor Robert Holmes designated a committee for the Study of the Problems of the Aged. Robert Miller, OTR, was appointed to that committee.

2. The annual conference of the American Occupational Therapy Association was held in Cleveland, Ohio on October 21-25. This conference was called the Institute Conference. One of the issues addressed by the national association at this conference was that there was a need to determine the boundaries between occupational therapy and physical therapy.

3. The 9th Western International Conference of Occupational and Physical Therapy was held in Vancouver, B.C., May 11-12. The theme of the conference was "Changing Concepts in Occupational and Physical Therapy".

4. An Institute for occupational therapists sponsored by the American Hospital Association was cancelled for lack of support. The Institute was to be held in Seattle. The theme was "Organization and Administration".

1958*

President: Elizabeth Callahan

Vice President: Elizabeth Irle

Secretary: Jean Vann

Treasurer: Dorothy Richards

Delegate: Mary Boyce

Major Events:

1. Marjorie Fish, OTR, Executive Director of the American Occupational Therapy Association visited the Oregon therapists.

2. The forty-first annual conference of the American Occupational Therapy Association was held in New York City. It was announced that there are 4,602 members of the association.

3. The 10th annual Western International Conference of Occupational and Physical Therapy was held May 17-18, 1958.

1959*

President: Elizabeth Callahan

Vice President: Elizabeth Irle

Secretary: Jean Vann

Treasurer: Dorothy Richards

Delegate: Mary Boyce

Major Events:

1. The first revision of the constitution of the association since it was founded in 1947 was completed. A vote of thanks was given to Grace Black for her work on this task.

2. Sister Jean Marie, R.N., OTR, started an occupational therapy department at Sacred Heart General Hospital in Eugene, Oregon.

4. Irene Hollis, OTR, visited the occupational therapy departments in Oregon during the month of March. She was the field consultant in rehabilitation for the American Occupational Therapy Association.

5. The 11th annual Western International Conference of Occupational and Physical Therapy was held in Seattle on May 2, 1959. The theme of the conference was "Geriatrics".

4
Certified Occupational Therapy Assistant (COTA) School: 1960-1967

Mt. Hood. © Aaron R. Proctor, OTD, OTR/L, Pacific University Class of 2015. Used with permission.

1960*

President: Dorothy Richards

Vice President: Flora Barrows

Secretary: Norma Holliman

Treasurer: Janice Clark

Delegate: Mary Boyce

Alternate Delegate: Virginia Hatch

Major Events:

1. A decision was made to send a monthly newsletter to the membership of the association. It was to contain meeting notices and agenda and other information of interest. This was to be sent by the Secretary.

2. Program suggestions for membership meetings were as follows:

    A trip to Goodwill Industries

    Demonstration of splints

    A topic related to Psychiatry

    Activities of Daily Living

3. The annual conference of the American Occupational Therapy Association was held in Los Angeles, California, in November.

1961*

President: Dorothy Richards

Vice President: Pat Evans

Secretary: Norma Holliman

Treasurer: James Nelson

Delegate/Alternate Delegate: Mary Boyce/Virginia Hatch

Major Events:

1. A salary study was compiled in May (a comparison of salaries of occupational therapists and treatment fees in the Portland area.) There was an occupational therapy exhibit at the Oregon Tuberculosis and Health Association annual meeting. There was an occupational therapy exhibit and recruitment materials at OMSI Career Day. Approximately 1,000 high school students were contacted.

2. A one-half hour television program on Channel 8, Portland, featured Margaret Linton, OTR, University of Oregon Medical School and an affiliating occupational therapy student. They discussed occupational therapy training, goals, and demonstrated self-help devices.

3. OTAO contacted the Governor's Committee on Mental Health to offer assistance with mental health planning in the state. Dammasch State Hospital opened. Wenda Lloyd, OTR, was the Occupational Therapy Director. A pre-therapy course was started at Williamette University. Dr. Gale Currey, RPT, was the director.

4. The 13th annual Western International Conference of Occupational and Physical Therapy was held in Portland at the Memorial Coliseum. Elizabeth Callahan, OTR, was the

coordination chairman. The theme of the conference was "Broadening Horizons in OT and PT".

5. OTAO Standard Committee complied craft information for nursing homes.

History of the OTA Program at Mt. Hood Community College

In the early 1960's a survey developed by the Oregon State Health Division was circulated throughout the state to longterm care facilities. The purpose of the survey was to assess the interest and need for occupational therapy in nursing homes. Reportedly, there was a "good response", and the Health Division developed the OT Nursing Home Project as a result of that survey. Jim Nelson OTR/L (who was employed at the Oregon State Health Division, Chronic Disease Section) helped develop and teach in the 36-hour project for occupational therapists to receive orientation and consultation to provide OT to patients and staff at longterm care facilities. As a result of this project, an acute awareness of the marked shortage of trained occupational therapy personnel moved Jim Nelson to further action. He created the Committee for the Development of the Certified Occupational Therapy Assistant. The occupational therapists who served on the committee included: Jim Nelson, Clara Smithhisler, Bonnie Harwood, and Jean Vann. The information gathering and work accomplished by this committee led to the development of the COTA program at Mt. Hood Community College (MHCC) in Gresham, Oregon. This was the first and only OTA educational program in the state. The nine month certification program opened in September 1967.

Walt Ludke OTR/L, was the first coordinator of the OTA program and served in that position form 1967-1977. The OTA program was the second health related program in the Allied Health Division and the Licensed Practical Nurse (LPN) was the first. Walt was also responsible for developing the Medical Terminology course (a requirement for Allied Health students.) He reported, "The first OTA courses were taught in an old abandoned tire shop in Gresham. The college was in a great state of change and classes were later taught in trailers on the college campus and room assignments were always changing."

The growth and development of community colleges continued

throughout the late 1960's and 1970's as well as the need for occupational therapy practitioners, OTR and COTA. During this time the American Occupational Therapy Association Commission on Education revised the essentials for OT curriculum which had a big impact on the role of the COTA. Across the nation, OTA programs were evolving to two-year Associate Degrees. In 1967 the OTA program at MHCC began due to a need for trained personnel who could provide direct services to patients, particularly the adult and aged population. Once again, the needs developed, and in 2010 Linn Benton Community College responded by developing and implementing a two-year Associate Degree OTA program.

In 1977, Lilian Crawford MOT, OTR/L, FAOTA was hired as a curriculum consultant by MHCC to develop course outlines, behavioral objectives and evaluation methods for a two-year Associate Degree OTA curriculum, as well as complete the Report of Compliance for AOTA. The first students for the two-year Associate Degree program were admitted Fall term 1977.

At that time (1977) the newly developed two-year curriculum was implemented and Lilian became the second OTA Program Director. She served in that position until 1984. Many occupational therapists including Jean Vann, Grace Malpass, Brana Mater, Keeston Lowery, Marian Neevel, Kay Rhoney, Karen Foley, and Linda Butery and Certified Occupational Therapy Assistants John Wirth and Sherry Dickens taught the OTA students and brought "real life" stories to their teaching since they all were also employed in various clinical environments. During that time, the role and definition of the COTA was "catching on" and their value as effective direct service professionals of occupational therapy made a big impact (developing programs in community mental health centers, longterm care facilities, etc.) In addition to classroom activities the students were active participants in professional organizations (OTAO and AOTA). During the 1980-1982 academic years, the students researched the development of OT in Oregon (OTAO) and interviewed many therapists who participated in developing the state OT association. That work resulted in writing and presenting [their] findings in a publication *Reflections: The History of the Occupational Therapy Association of Oregon (1947-1981)*.

The 1983 AOTA National Conference, which was held in Portland, brought more opportunity for the OTA students. They made up the entire student committee for the conference and were recognized for their enthusiastic and professional work (hosting all students who attended conference.) One of the OT's who was in attendance at that conference was Chris Heideman (Hencinski) MS, OTR/L. She was inquiring about a possible teaching position and was recruited for the OTA Program Director position. Chris was the third and last OTA Program Director, serving from September 1984 – June 2003. Other OTA faculty Kathleen Hannigan-McNamara OTR/L CCT and Sue Byers-Connon MS COTA/L. They reported that all passed the certification exam and found employment upon graduation. The SOTA club was especially active and found students volunteering with Meals on Wheels, leading activity-based groups in assisted living facilities and participating in Providence Festival of Trees (annual fundraising event for Providence Child Care Center). Many students attended both the state and national conferences and several students were elected to SOTA positions at the national level. At the turn of the century (2000) the OTA Program, like others throughout the nation, experienced a "dip" in applications and as a result had low enrollment. The President of MHCC at that time (Dr. Robert Silverman) took note and chose to discontinue the program as an expedient way to address some of the college wide budget issues. The last class graduated from the program in June 2003.

—**Lilian Crawford**

Our profession has undergone amazing changes in regards to settings, populations, legislative measures, insurance coverage for treatment, licensure, and salaries within the last 100 years. Below is a glimpse of common salaries in the state of Oregon. This information was used to recruit new members to the profession during outreach events.

COMPARISON OF MONTHLY/ANNUAL SALARIES PAID TO OCCUPATIONAL THERAPISTS AND TREATMENT FEES CHARGED IN THE PORTLAND OREGON AREA.*

COMPILED MAY 1961 FOR THE OCCUPATIONAL THERAPY ASSOCIATION OF OREGON

PRIVATE INSTITUTIONS	CHIEF THERAPIST	STAFF THERAPIST	ANNUAL INCREASE
Morningside Hospital	$450	$350 – $425	$20 – $25
Holladay Park Hospital	(none)	$350	$10/mo.
Rehabilitation Institute of Oregon	$375	$350	(none setup)
PUBLIC SCHOOLS			
Portland, OR	(none)	$3700 – $5900 (9 mo.)	$200/yr.
Vancouver, WA	(none)	$4000 – $5650	$200/yr.
STATE OF OREGON	$4560 – 5760 OT II	$4320 – 5280 OT I	
U.S. GOVERNMENT			
Veterans Administration	$6435 – $7425 (GS-9)	$5355 – $6345 (GS-6)	$165
	$5885 – $6875 (GS-8)	$4345 – $5335 (GS-5)	

TREATMENT FEES	TYPE OF TREATMENT	FEE
Visiting Therapists	Orthopedic, largely	$6.00/treatment
Rehabilitation Institute of Oregon	Orthopedic	$6.00/treatment
Holladay Park Hospital	GM & S	$5.00/hr.
	Psychiatric – OT fee is included in the per diem rate – approx. $0.50 per day, per patient	
University-State Tuberculosis Hospital	Tuberculosis – Patient pays cost of materials or makes duplicate article for OT department sale	

1962*

President: Pat Evans

Vice President: Jan Vroman

Secretary: Ariji Lietuvietis

Treasurer: Dixie Arata

Delegate: Betty Irle

Alternate Delegate: Elizabeth Callahan

Major Events:

1. Due to extensive mailing costs, the newsletter no longer was sent to each therapists home. One copy was sent to each occupational therapy department. However, at-home therapists still received their copies through the mail.

2. Bernice See, OTR, was interviewed on Channel KATU (2). She discussed occupational therapy on the "Northwest Living" program.

3. Jeanne Haase, OTR, begins the occupational therapy program at Emanuel Hospital.

4. The annual meeting of the association was held May 9, 1962. Seven certified occupational therapy assistants (certified in psychiatry) were given special recognition at the banquet.

6. A Career Day was held on April 14th at the University of Oregon Medical School Hospital. Approximately 250 high school juniors and seniors visited the occupational therapy portion of the event.

7. The 14th annual Western International Conference of Occupational and Physical Therapy was held on April 28th in

Seattle. The theme was "Current Concepts in Treating the Handicapped Child".

The day to day of occupational therapy in the 1960's included much work outside of the clinical context. It was up to volunteer efforts of OTAO members to charter publicity, education, recruitment, and fund raising. In addition, it acted as a peer support group and opportunity for occupational therapists to engage interpersonally.

This letter demonstrates some unique contributions of OTAO members and acts as inspiration for others to seek involvement. The below document describes creative ways OTAO used members' meaningful occupations as a method to raise funds. Jean Vann worked tirelessly to document these types of fundraising efforts in order create a historical account of the efforts sustained by proactive OTAO members.

January 21, 1962

HIGHTLIGHTS AND HAPPENINGS OF THE OCCUPATIONAL THERAPY ASSOCIATION OF OREGON

Publicity was spread by JoAnn Freimund and Maggie Drake with a stations wagon with six preschool kids in it. They visited all the high schools with one person taking a turn at sitting the kids in the station wagon while the other went into the high school to talk with counselors and leave literature. Therapists at home formed a group which met at various homes, but most often at JoAnn Freimund's home, as she had a fenced backyard with play equipment and the most preschool children (4). At these meetings, children's clothing and baby equipment were exchanged (also maternity clothes). Recipes were also exchanged. Recent developments in occupational therapy were discussed. Much volunteer work of OTAO was done by this group. Some went into the State Nursing Home Project. One of the highlights of these meetings was Sue Nelson bringing an occupational therapist from Bombay, India to a meeting.

Some of the fund raising projects included: Since OTAO

membership was small, fundraisers as a rule had to depend upon general public. A large 21" baby doll with a complete layette was raffled for a few times. The raffle winner was a pregnant woman who had a small baby who could wear the layette. Other projects included anything that could be profitably raffled was raffled. Home OT's made and sold baked goods to working OTs at meetings, Flav-R-Pac labels were saved and turned in, Civic Theater tickets were sold for plays, a health booklet was sold, and an OT Mobile (designed at the V.A. in Vancouver) was sold.

ATPO (Associated Therapists, Physical and Occupational) was formed when Medicare came into being to handle demands for home health agencies to have occupational and physical therapy. With advice of Clem Eischen's uncle, a non-profit corporation was formed with Clancy Hultgren, RPT, as president and Jean Vann, OTR, as secretary-treasurer. I believe Wilbur Gregory was the third officer. This group negotiated contracts, advised for salaries, and maintained standards. Talks were held with Multnomah County Home Health Agency, Portland Home Health Agency, Associated Home Health Agency, Vising Nurse Association, and Permanente. Contracts were also signed with Washington County Home Health Agency, Clackamas County Home Health Agency, and Columbia County Home Health Agency. This group was phased out of business when the home health agencies grew large enough to hire a part-time therapist, and the Oregon State Board of Health adopted a contract to be used by the agencies within the state. The contract was worked up by the State and ATPO. A state nursing home project was spearheaded by Dr. William Wright of the Chronic Disease section of the Oregon State Board of Health with Margaret Prior, RPT, and Jim Nelson, OTR. This project endeavored to bring some rehabilitation techniques and activities to nursing home residents. Occupational and Physical Therapists from all over the state participated, and were assigned to nursing homes requesting to be included in this project.

—Jean Vann

The following letter was written by Dottie Richards, former OTAO president. It was important during these days to recruit new members and this letter acts as a good example of how OT professionals can vary their degree of involvement within the organization. Membership continues to be a challenge today. According to Nancy Schuberg, Oregon OT Licensing Board, there are currently 1,896 registered occupational therapist and 469 registered certified occupational therapy assistants (Nov. 2016).

OCCUPATIONAL THERAPY ASSN. of OREGON

January 5, 1962

Hello:

As one occupational therapist to another, I hope you will lend an ear for just a few minutes to listen to something that is of real concern to all of us therapists here in Oregon.

Do you realize that there are at least 50 qualified therapists in the Oregon area (that includes Vancouver and Longview, Washington too) but only 29 of these are current members of the Occupational Therapy Association of Oregon? Forty-two are members of AOTA and 45 maintain registration, but twenty of you aren't in the ranks of the Oregon group (OTAO) and we want you with us. If you aren't against us, you must be for us, and for $3.00 a year we could be of mutual benefit to each other.

We would like you to visit one of our meetings occasionally, even if you don't care to attend regularly. You won't be put to work unless you wish to (although there are a surprising number of ways you could help us, even in your own home if you had an hour or two now and then that you could spare for telephoning, assembling recruitment packets, etc.) Mainly, though, we just like to see you once in a while to chit-chat and let you listen in on what goes on in the local OT departments.

And, of course, your financial support would mean a lot to us. We in the OTAO feel that Oregon must be represented at the AOTA National Convention, and we have been scraping the barrel to send our delegate for the past 4 years. We try to pay the equivalent of air coach fare to the conference city, and 1962's trip to Philadelphia will cost us about $301.95.

This is our major expense, but last year we also were active in state, regional and local workshops and conferences, which cost us money also. We have a traveling recruitment exhibit which we use at various health fairs and meetings; we sponsored a psychiatric workshop in Salem, and sent our representatives to a recruitment workshop in Seattle, as well as to some local publicity meets. We do get around locally, too – meeting with State Civil Service Commission, Multnomah County Council for the Aging, Emergency Medical Service Committee of the Oregon State Medical Society, joint meetings with the Oregon Chapter of Physical Therapists, etc. So your membership support would help our state association maintain its present professional status and go forward in the community.

Recruitment has always been a problem, and is currently our big concern. We have good plans for the coming year, but handout leaflets and brochures are expensive, and we need enthusiastic promoters who will volunteer to speak for high schools and other key groups.

To meet our budget we have to count on one main fundraising activity . . . and dues! Last year we sponsored a Civic Theater Blue Room production. This year's project hasn't been decided – we have a date for a rummage sale in 1963! But whatever it is we have to rely heavily on full-hearted support and a full paid-up membership. Our group is small, but amongst us we have what it takes to get the job done – that is, if we can count on everyone.

IF YOU CAN'T GIVE US YOUR TIME, WE'LL TAKE YOUR DIME

Thanks for listening. Come see us when you can . . . (you get the newsletter, don't you?) And do send us $3.00 right away — you'll be glad you did.

Sincerely,

Dorothy E. Richards, OTR, President

OCCUPATIONAL THERAPY ASSOCIATION OF OREGON

*This is a copy of a letter sent by the president of OTAO to therapists in the state encouraging them to join the state association.

This is a copy of a letter sent to AOTA accepting the invitation to host the 1968 national conference. This was the first of two national OT conferences held in Oregon.

January 21, 1962

Miss G. Margaret Gleave, OTR

Permanent Conference Chairman
American Occupational Therapy Association
2335 Northwestern Avenue
Racine, Wisconsin

Dear Miss Gleave:

The American Occupational Therapy Association of Oregon has voted unanimously to accept the privilege and challenge of hosting the 1968 conference. We hope that we have not exceeded the deadline for your decision.

We would be happy to have the conference in Portland and feel that we have excellent facilities. These include a recently build Sheraton Hotel and Memorial Coliseum which were the scene of the 1962 Association of Western Hospitals Conference. Both of these buildings are located near our famous shopping center, "The Lloyd Center". In addition, there are several hotels in the downtown area, including a new Hilton, which would be large enough to accommodate the conference.

Our enthusiasm for the conference stems from the fact we have successfully hosted the Western International Conference of Occupational and Physical Therapists every third year (the other two years being held in Vancouver, B. C. and a city in Washington). We feel that the conference would be a great benefit to the Portland-Vancouver (Washington) area and to the whole Northwest in educating both the medial profession and lay people in the potential of Occupational Therapy. It would help to have the spotlighting of our large national conference as we do not have an OT school in Oregon.

Any further questions from you will be welcomed most heartily, and we will try to answer them as quickly as possible.

Sincerely,

Mrs. Patricia Evans, OTR
President, OTAO

1963*

President: Jean Vann

Vice President: Norma Holliman

Secretary: Jean Haase

Treasurer: Ann Egbert

Delegate/Alternate Delegate: Betty Irle/ Elizabeth Callahan

Major Events:

1. OTAO dues were $5.00 for working therapists, $3.00 for non-working therapists, and $1.50 for aides. OTAO annual meeting was held March 9, 1963 at the Mayfair House Restaurant.

2. The 15th annual Western International Conference of Occupational and Physical Therapy was held at the Bayshore Inn, Vancouver, British Columbia. The theme of the conference was "The Time Has Come". Due to the defeat of a state tax measure, the occupational therapy positions with the state were "shaky". There were no positions in OT available for the first time in years.

3. The Multnomah County Council on the Aging held their first annual meeting on January 29, 1963. It was presented by the Housing Authority of Portland and Friendly House, Inc. There was a "huge" snow storm in Portland on that day also.

4. Melinda Wayne, OTR, begins the occupational therapy department at Edgefield Manor. The annual AOTA conference was held October 1-4 in St. Louis, Missouri. The theme of the conference was, "Time to Climb".

5. OTAO held a Technique Fair on April 9th at Morningside Hospital. There were many demonstrations by therapists of

occupational therapy techniques. The objective of the fair was recruitment. OTAO looked into the possibility of starting an Occupational Therapy Assistant Program in Oregon.

1964*

President: Jean Vann

Vice President: Connie Weiss

Secretary: Nancy Woodruff

Treasurer: Jean Haase

Delegate/ Alternate Delegate: Elizabeth Callahan/ Ruth Pray

Major Events:

1. Bob Miller, OTR, was appointed to the State Mental Health Planning Board. The second Seminar on Rehabilitation was held at Emanuel Hospital on March 12, 1964. The speakers included Howard Rusk, M.D., New York, and Wilbert Fordyce, PhD., Seattle.

2. O.T.A.O. contacted Mike Tichy, PhD., Physical Education Department of Portland State, about the possibility of beginning an Occupational Therapy School. It was suggested the facilities at the University of Oregon Medical School could be used.

3. O.T.A.O. participated in the televised lessons for nursing home aides titled, "Aids for Aides". This was sponsored by the Division of Continuing Education and Oregon State Board of Health and shown on Channel 10. The annual conference of the American Occupational Therapy Association was held in Denver, Colorado, in October. This conference included the premiere of the recruitment film, "To Pick A Life". Wilma L. West, OTR was president of the association.

4. The 16th annual Western International Conference of Occupational and Physical Therapy was held at the Sheraton Motor Inn, Portland on April 25, 1964. The topics included

Spinal Cord Injuries and Strokes. Mary Fender, OTR (new graduate) started the occupational therapy department at Portland Sanitarium (Portland Adventist) Hospital. Columbia View Manor was looking for an occupational therapist for their facility.

1965*

President: Connie Weiss

Vice President: Jan Clark

Secretary: Judy Rowe

Treasurer: Marilyn Forse (also Helen Metcalf)

Delegate/Alternate Delegate: Jean Vann/ Ruth Pray

Major Events:

1. O.T.A.O. Membership was 51 (29 active therapists, 12 at home therapists, 10 associate members).

2. O.T.A.O. annual meeting was held at the Hillvilla Restaurant on April 23. Jean Vann was honored as "Lady of the Year". She was presented with a crown and a lei as well as joke books and jewelry from Tiffany's.

3. Fund raising projects for this year included saving Flavor-pac-labels, a rummage sale, buying season tickets for the opera, and selling hand designed stationary.

4. The "home" therapists (Jean Vann, Marilyn Forse, Wenda Lloyd, and Ruth Ann Moore) gathered at Jean's home to work on the hand designed stationery. They were sold for $2.50 per dozen.

5. The annual conference of the American Occupational Therapy Association was held in Miami, Florida. Ruth Brunyate, OTR was president. O.T.A.O. began planning for the 1968 A.O.T.A. conference which was scheduled for Portland.

6. A course on Research was offered at Portland State Univ. Interested therapists were to contact Joan Freimund, OTR. The 17th annual Western International Conference of

Occupational and Physical Therapy was held at the Hyatt House in Seattle on May 1, 1965. The theme of the conference was "Current Trends in Health Care."

1966*

President: Judy Rowe

Vice President: Nancy Parrish

Secretary: Ruth Peterson

Treasurer: Marilyn Forse

Delegate: Jean Vann

Alternate Delegate: Dixie Arata

Major Events:

1. There was an occupational therapy exhibit in the Biology Wing of OMSI. Jan Clark, Lois Walsh, and Carol Page were responsible for the exhibit.

2. Linda Johnson, OTR, started the occupational therapy program at the Robison Home.

3. Medicare was a major issue during 1966. A committee of therapists met to implement occupational therapy for Medicare patients.

4. Members of OTAO viewed the AOTA recruitment film "Target".

1967*

President: Judy Rowe

Vice President: Linda Johnson

Secretary: Carol Ayles

Treasurer: Ruth Rollins

Delegate: Jean Vann

Alternate Delegate: Dixie Arata

Major Events:

1. OTAO supports the Oregon State Board of Health's Application for a federally funded Health Manpower Data Center.

2. The Pacific Regional Conference of the National Rehabilitation Association is held at the Sheraton Hotel in Portland. The theme of the conference is "New Services in Rehabilitation".

3. The Occupational Therapy Assistant Program at Mt. Hood Community College began in September 1967. It began as a nine month certification course with Walt Ludtke, OTR as director.

4. Dues for OTAO during this year were $7.00 for working therapists, $4.00 for home therapists, and $2.00 for associates. Dues for AOTA during this year were $30.00 for OTR, $10.00 for COTA, and $7.50 for students.

5. The annual conference of the American Occupational Therapy Association was held in Boston, Massachusetts. This year marked the 50th anniversary of the association and the theme of the conference was "Historical Perspectives – the AOTA". A proposal was made at the conference to change the name of

the profession to Teleo-Therapy. Teleo means to accomplish a purpose, to perform, to do.

6. The 19th annual Western International Conference of Occupational and Physical Therapy was held at the Benson Hotel in Portland. The topics included aphasia, amputations, arthritis, and geriatrics. McKenzie W. Buck, PhD., was one of the speakers.

8. Dixie Arata, OTR, started a woodworking and homemaking skills program at Haugh School in Vancouver for MR/DD teenagers.

9. The annual meeting of OTAO was held at Eve's Restaurant on May 23, 1967.

5
Rehabilitation Institute of Oregon (RIO) Development: 1968-1976

Budding Flower. © Martha Wegner, OTD, OTR/L, Pacific University Class of 2015. Used with permission.

1968*

President: Walt Ludtke

Vice President: Carol Sutherland

Secretary: Jean Haase

Treasurer: Ruth Rawlins

Delegate: Jean Vann

Alternate Delegate: Dixie Arata

Major Events:

1. The annual conference for the American Occupational Therapy Association was held in Portland. The theme was "Reaching for Peaks". Mary Boyce, OTR was conference planning chairman.

2. The 20th annual Western International Conference of Occupational and Physical Therapy was held at the University of Puget Sound, Tacoma, Washington, on May 4, 1968. The topic of the conference was congenital defects.

3. Medicare was a major issue during 1966. A committee of therapists met to implement occupational therapy for Medicare patients.

This is an illustrated promotional poster for the first national AOTA conference held in Portland, Oregon. The illustrator remains unknown. The conference was held in the fall of 1968 and included five full days of events, exhibits, speakers, etc. AOTA Publication.

AOTA PRELIMINARY PROGRAM – 1968

Monday, October 21, 1968

Tours

Tuesday, October 22, 1968

3:00 – 5:00   Opening of Exhibits

7:00 – 10:00 Films

Wednesday, October 23, 1968

9:30 – 10:00 Breakfast – Washington Occupational Therapy Association

10:00   Keynote Speech – Research Peaks

1:30 – 2:30   Legal Liability in Practice of O.T. – General Session

2:45 – 5:00   Two Concurrent Sessions –

1. Panel on Philosophy of Rehabilitation and Relocation in Industry – composed of an OTR, psychologist, industrialist, and labor union representative

2. Panel on neurological disorders and their implications

Thursday, October 24, 1968

9:00 – 12:00 Two Concurrent Sessions –

1. 1. Curriculum Research and Development

2. Research and Development for Practice

3. Latest Developments in Perceptual Motor Dysfunction

2:00 – 4:30   Two Concurrent Sessions –

1. Presentation on Neuromuscular Facilitation

2. Presentation emphasizing psychiatric research

4:30 – 5:15   Ships Drawing

7:00   Banquet

Friday, October 25, 1968

9:00 – 9:45   Two Concurrent Sessions

1. Neurological Effects on the CVA patients

2. Prove or Disprove the Value of Maintenance Therapy

10:00 – 10:45   Two Concurrent Sessions

1. The Aphasic Patient

   2. Communication Problems in Administration

11:00 – 11:45   Two Concurrent Sessions

   1. Presentation on Geriatric Advances

   2. Oregon's Participation with Home Health Agencies for Medicare

12:00 – 2:00   Luncheon

2:15   Annual Business Meeting

OTAO and the Rehabilitation Institute of Oregon (RIO) are two organizations that would not exist without each other. RIO remains very influential to the profession today while incorporating evidenced-based practice methods and developing research within a neurodevelopmental rehabilitation setting. The below document is a history of RIO; formerly named The Portland Rehabilitation Center.

Published by the RIO Guild in appreciation of the efforts of Mrs. Roy R. Clark in pioneering in the field of rehabilitation. The author is unknown.

May 28, 1968

JULY 1947, "it is timely now to go ahead". And thus began the series of events that eventually led to the establishment of the Rehabilitation Institute of Oregon – first named Portland Rehabilitation Center.

It unofficially began however, in the spring of 1947 when dramatic photographs of a local group of severely handicapped persons who met regularly in a "Chin Up Club" moved Portlanders to seek further help for these disabled persons. At about the same time, the Easter Seal Society conducted its first drive in Oregon and indicated an interest in a program of rehabilitation for the handicapped.

As the first move to get the project underway, Howard Feast, executive director of the Oregon Society for Crippled Children and Adults, met with a citizens' committee including Dr. Ernest J. Jaqua, ex-president of Scripps college and former educational secretary of the Baruch committee on physical medicine. Dr. Jaqua had traveled widely helping to establish training centers for therapists to be used in army hospitals. As a result of this meeting, Dr. and Mrs. Jaqua later moved to Portland from the farm in Southern Oregon where they had retired, to assist in planning for a rehabilitation facility.

The Gold Room of the Portland Hotel, June, 1947, was the setting for a meeting of an informal committee of about twelve who met over lunch to elect Dr. Jaque chairman and lay plans for the organization. Arthur Jones, M.D., who was to play a key role in the institution for several years to come, was also present. He had just returned from service in World War II – most recently from Letterman Army Hospital where he had been director of Rehabilition and Physical Medicine.

The United Fund urged that a state-wide survey of needs and facilities in the area of rehabilitation be undertaken as a necessary stage in the planning.

A July, 1947, newspaper account tells us the "medical, social, government leaders met to discuss a rehabilitation center for Oregon" at the Medical-Dental building under the auspices of the Oregon Society for Crippled Children and Adults. Representatives of Goodwill, Welfare, D.V.R., and the United Fund were also present.

The newspaper story tells us that the group agreed "it is timely now to go ahead with such a project." And the account goes on to say that Dr. Jaqua was named chairman of a fact-finding committee of six who would survey the state's needs.

And so the work began. The Society pledged $20,000 to the center, and gave office space to be used for the project while it was being organized.

By June, 1948, the first formal board meeting was held at the Mallory Hotel with Gordon Orput as chairman. Dr. Jaqua's committee report documenting the need for a rehabilitation facility was presented. Dr. Jones introduced two therapists – the first staff members for the institution. Chairman Orput reported on the successful search for a location for the center: a large old house at 11th and Montgomery formerly used as a rooming house. The board voted to rent and adapt the house for RIO's use. (The name was changed from Portland Rehabilitation Center to RIO after the move to Kearney St.)

Mrs. Roy Clark had just returned from a visit to centers in Toronto, Boston, New York, Milwaukee, and Virginia and reported on these programs.

The summer of 1948 was an extremely busy time for the group of dedicated volunteers who were determined to open a facility for the handicapped. Donations from more than 50 firms and individuals were received by Board Chairman Orput and his board members. These included tools for the shop from Marshall Wells, a few pieces of therapy equipment, and drapery materials from Meier and Frank. Meier and Frank also loaned the services of a decorator who worked with volunteers in making draperies for the entire building. A local contractor donated $3,000 worth of renovation – tearing out the cubicles in the basement used by roomers, moving partitions and other necessary structural changes. The same firm also build ramps at the front and back for use by wheel chair patients. Even the two therapists busied themselves by tearing off old wallpaper. The volunteers then replaced the wallpaper.

NOVEMEBER 19, 1948, in site of a severe storm, more than 200 Portlanders turned out for the open house at the new rehabilitation center, including Mayor Dorothy McCullock Lee. Governor Tom McCall, then a reporter for the Oregonian, covered the event. A cheerful fire burned in the handsome fireplace in the entry hall, and Christmas greens festooned the paneled lounge. A large wreath decorated the stair landing. That night the center admitted its first patient through Dr. Jones, who had by that time been named part-time Medical Director.

A temporary director was recruited through one of the board members, Dr. Richard Steiner, pastor of the First Unitarian Church. One of his parishioners, Mrs. Emma Rekate, had recently resigned her position after 22 years as secretary to E.B. McNaughton, president of the First National Bank. Mrs. Rekate capably managed the affairs of the institute until Miss Winifred Roby (now Mrs. Herman Becker) was employed. Miss Roby was a physical therapist who had formerly held an executive position at a large mid-Western hospital. During the first year with the center she not only acted as director, but also did bookkeeping, typing and answered necessary correspondence. Later these duties were transferred to other staff, but during those first months Miss Roby wore many hats.

The second year at 11th and Montgomery, the Easter Seal Society's national policy changed and called for control of any project to which the society had allocated funds. The dedicated board of directors however, refused to allow direction of the project to be transferred to a national association. At the end of the second year the Society for Crippled Children and Adults withdrew its financial assistance form the center. Fortunately, the Department of Vocational Rehabilitation had become interested in the program and sent many of its handicapped clients to the institution. With this continuing help over several years, the center continued to grow. The Community Chest, through Dr. Jaqua who had become a member of its board, offered to add the center to the list of agencies it supported. And although the allocation was small and has not increased over the years, board members have felt the importance of the United Fund support.

As the patient load grew, the quarters at 11th and Montgomery became increasingly inadequate, and a search was begun for a new building. After considering several properties, the board voted to purchase a large building at 14th and Mill streets. The building itself was just a shell – it had no furnace, no ceilings and only rough concrete walls. But it offered space and was located at an attractive site surrounded by large old trees.

Again a community-wide effort raised the down payment in addition to another $20,000 for renovation of the building. At this critical moment, some of RIO's friends came forward with substantial gifts: Aaron Frank, Gordon Orput, Mr. and Mrs. E.C. Sammons, Hall Templeton, Mrs. Orville Miller, Julius Zell, the late Philip Fields, and many others. The unions in the community were also brought into the project by chairman of the board Gordon Orput. Installation of floor and wall coverings, necessary partitions, labor and materials were donated through the unions. At the same time, many business firms and contractors also supplied necessary materials.

Upon the recommendations of the professional staff, it was decided that a pool would enhance the treatment program. The Junior League made a substantial donation toward the contruction of the addition to the building, the two pools and hydro-therapy equipment. The Hod Carriers and Brick Layers Unions donated most of the labor for pool wing, amounting to many thousands of dollars. Several women's groups in the city also came forward with donations including the Women of Elks, Women of Rotary, Soroptimists, and several sororities.

A newspaper account dated December 13, 1952, describes the new property as including "two structures; a two-story and single story building forming an L around a 100 x 100 foot lot. An addition to the present building is planned for part of the lot with parking and open-air therapy for the remainder. The new center will have a swimming pool, gymnasium, offices, manual arts, physical and occupational therapy, whirl-pool baths and other aids to rehabilitate persons crippled from accidents of diseases such as polio."

In JUNE, 1953, the rehabilitation center moved to the Mill Street building, then largely completed, which was to be its home for the next decade. In 1956, D.V.R. secured $15,000 in federal funds to adapt the second floor for a special treatment area. A most successful OT program; a complete shop; and a Cerebral Palsy evaluation center were housed there. The evaluation center received a grant from the U.S. Department of Health, and the local Cerebral Palsy chapter also contributed almost $10,000. This program was conducted by a member of the RIO staff, but after a year the C.P. Center moved to the Double OO Workshop where

| 83

training for employment was given. The center has remained there as a money-raising program for Cerebral Palsy victims whose progress has largely become stabilized.

Often beset by financial problems, RIO's work went on with many notable successes with severely handicapped patients during this decade. In April, 1954, an open hosue was held attended by friends and supporters, as well as the board of directors and staff.

On MAY 23, 1958, the women's guild was founded with Mrs. Jean Young as the first president. The guild dedicated itself to fund-raising projects to enhance patient care at the institution. The women also busied themselves with birthday parties for patients and the like.

Another important step forward in August, 1958, was the painting of the exterior of the concrete building by volunteers from the Avondale Contracting Company. This added a great deal to the appearance of the structure, and no doubt enhanced its value when it was later purchased by the Highway Commission.

One of the many persons who gave his moral support and enthusiastic encouragement was Admiral Ross McIntyre, whose name was a household word because he had been President Franklin D. Roosevelt's personal physician. He twice visited the center during his travels across the country from Washington, D.C., once shortly after the doors opened and the second time after the center had moved to the 14th and Mill location.

THE TENTH ANNIVERSARY of the founding of R.I.O. was celebrated with a gala dinner sponsored by the guild on November 19, 1958. Governor Tom McCall, then a member of the Oregonian staff and always a good friend of R.I.O. was master-of-ceremonies. Several of Portland's prominent citizens and the many donors who had helped develop the center was honored at this time.

It became apparent that the building was becoming inadequate-

chiefly because only out-patients could be treated and because maintenance problems became serious – so the Board of Directors again began a search for better quarters. At about the same time, the Highway Commission began negotiating for property which would be needed for the projected Stadium Freeway. At first there was no hint that the center would be displaced, and indeed the freeway itself was in doubt since the community was sharply divided over the plan to bisect the core area. When the Highway Commission presented its final plans, it was evident that the Rehabilitation Center would have to move. The commission offered about $187,500 for the land; the building had no bargaining value. This was slightly more than twice the $90,000 originally paid for the land and building by the center.

In JULY, 1961, the board of directors took an option to buy the present building at 20th and Kearney, and in December, 1961, the equipment was moved out and the old building was closed. Meanwhile, Dr. V.E. Mikkelson had been appointed the first full-time medical director for the institute. An Oregonian editorial titled "Kicked Out and UP" pointed to the fact that the Highway Commission gave R.I.O. a "welcome assist" by routing the new freeway through the property and purchasing the land. R.I.O. was able to make "a substantial down payment" the editorial stated on the Kearney Street Convalescent which could serve both in-patients and out-patients. "Increased income from the enlarged institute and from convalescent as well as rehabilitation patients, board members feel certain, will make possible both the payment of the debt and operation of the institute, complete with a full-time director." The editorial went on to state that Dr. Mikkelson had "serve his residency in physical medicine at the University of Oregon Medical School. . . and has practiced this branch of medicine both privately and with the Veterans Administration." In addition, John Munro had been a P.T. for several months and was very helpful in getting the in-patient service established.

After moving to the new building however, it was evident that more funds would be needed to finish and equip the building so it would be adaptable as an in-patient facility. Again, the guild proved both imaginative and helpful. One member secured a large quantity of china from Lipman's where management was changing the pattern used in the lunchroom. Another donated light fixtures in the lounge and gym. Gifts of many other articles or rebates on the prices of others made it possible to furnish the lounge. The Guild paid for most of the painting and arranged for a favorable price on floor coverings as well as the shutters in the lounge and the shades in the offices. The concrete floor installed in the lounge was financed from money left from the sale of the 14th and Mill property. After months of effort, the building became more livable, and the necessity of increasing the patient load to make the center operate in the black became obvious.

In 1965, R.I.O.'s allocation from UGN was sharply scrutinized by the UGN Finance Committee, and the question of community need for the institution again came to the fore. Dedicated R.I.O. board members convinced UGN that R.I.O.'s allocation should not be cut without an impartial survey into the matter. UGN hired a team: R.D. Burke, M.D., director of the Ohio Rehabilitation Center, Columbus; and T.P. Hipkens, director of the Home for Crippled Children, Pittsburgh Pa. These two men prepared a report that documented the need for a facility such as R.I.O. and the UGN allocation continued.

Following Dr. Mikkelson's tenure, another Physical Medicine specialist was employed, Dr. Albert Siegel, who after a brief stay returned to his home in the east. During the interim, John Monro's prudent handling of the finances of R.I.O. kep the institution doors open, and Dr. C.G. Loosli stepped in to fill the position of Medical Director part-time and served in that capacity until late in 1965. Dr. George Cottrell then served as part-time director until the appointment of the present full-time director, Dr. Leland Cross, in July, 1967.

Meanwhile, the imaginative and energetic guild continued their financial assistance to the institution by sponsoring the annual bridge parties that required months of telephoning and preparation. The annual tea at which the silver bowl bridge trophy was awarded became an important item on Portland's spring social calendar. As the personnel of the guild changed, so did the complexion of the fund-raising projects which ranged from rummage sales to the present day Sports Equipment Exchange – a sale of high quality formerly owned sports equipment. In June, 1967, a former president of the Guild, Mrs. Harold Cake, gave a luncheon at the Equitable Savings and Loan auditorium as a recognition of the valuable financial public relations contributions by the Guild.

One of the important steps in acquainting the medical community with the services offered by the Rehabilitation Institute was the establishment at the institute of an Amputee Clinic by F.A. Short, M.D., in 1962. Dr. Short remains in charge of the R.I.O. clinic, which has continued to grow in stature in the community.

Dr. Cross, who has come to head the institution from California where he was director of Physical Medicine and Rehabilitation at Los Angeles County Harbor General Hospital, has also been appointed assistant clinical professor of Neurology in rehabilitation at the University of Oregon Medical School. Under Dr. Cross's administration, the institution has begun to operate in the black for the first time in the past few years. Dr. Cross holds his M.D. from Northwestern and an M.P.H. from the University of California's graduate school.

As the institution continues to grow and prosper, the pioneering spirit of those dedicated Portlanders who foresaw the vital role of rehabilitation in medicine remains an inspiration to all Oregonians.

1969*

President: Walt Ludtke

Vice President: Carol Sutherland

Secretary: Jean Haase

Treasurer: Ruth Rawlins

Delegate: Jean Vann

Alternate Delegate: Dixie Arata

Major Events:

1. A workshop was held in May 1969 at Mt. Hood Community College entitled, "New-Help New Hope". The role of the Certified Occupational Therapy Assistant and the consultant in long term care were discussed.

2. The annual conference of the American Occupational Therapy Association was held in Dallas, Texas, November 2-7.

1970*

President: Linda Johnson

Vice President: Shirley Jackson

Secretary: Marilyn Forse

Treasurer: Edna Ellen Bell

Delegate: Dixie Arata

Major Events:

1. This was the first year that OTAO was listed in the phone book. This was the Reactivation Year for the American Occupational Therapy Association. Therapists who had let their certification lapse could return to registered status without retaking the registry exam.

2. Mrs. Harriet Tiebel, Executive Director of AOTA, testified before the Senate Finance Committee on its hearing on amendments to the Medicare Law and other provisions of the Social Security Act. The proposal was that occupational therapy services be authorized in home health care programs without the requirement that skilled nursing, physical therapy or speech therapy services first be authorized as a prerequisite. The issue of licensure was again being discussed. It was noted that this was an issue of great concern to therapists.

3. The annual conference of the American Occupational Therapy Association was held in New York City. The focus for this conference was Community Health.

4. An article entitled, "Oregon's Mental Patients: Are They Protected?" which appeared in the November 15, 1970 edition of NORTHWEST MAGAZINE of the OREGONIAN caused quite an uproar in the occupational therapy community. The article

stated that patients are required to work in the hospitals (run errands, scrub floors, clean toilets, etc.) and that this work is called occupational therapy.

1971*

President: Linda Johnson

Vice President: Dora Rice

Secretary: Flora Barrows

Treasurer: Edna Ellen Bell

Delegate: Dixie Arata

Major Events:

1. Community education was the priority of the association this year.

2. Bonnie Harwood, OTR, was on the Good Morning Show on Channel 2 discussing occupational therapy.

3. Walt Ludtke, OTR and Mary Boyce, OTR were on a committee to look into the possibility of developing a school of occupational therapy in Oregon.

4. Dr. Jacob of the University of Oregon Medical School spoke at the April meeting of the membership. The topic was DMSO.

5. The American Occupational Therapy Association was experiencing a staff crisis. It was becoming more and more difficult to recruit and hire staff who would choose to work in Manhattan. The question of moving the national office arose.

6. OTAO annual meeting was held at the Chinese Village on May 21, 1971.

1972*

President: Bonnie Harwood

Vice President: Sharon Loper

Secretary: Marilyn Forse

Treasurer: Maggie Drake

Delegate: Linda Johnson

Alternate Delegate: Judy Rowe

Major Events:

1. Certified Occupational Therapy Assistants became voting members of OTAO.

2. Many issues relating to the Certified Occupational Therapy Assistant were discussed this year. Two of these issues were the role of the COTA (especially in longterm care) and the possibility of changing the nine-month certificate program for training to a two year associate degree program.

3. The issue of licensure was again discussed by the membership.

1973*

President: Bonnie Harwood

Vice President: Janet Vroman

Secretary: Yvonne Johnson

(She was the first COTA to hold office in OTAO)

Treasurer: Sue Milton

Delegate: Linda Johnson

Alternate Delegate: Judy Rowe

Major Events:

1. A committee to study and make recommendations regarding architectural barriers was started.

2. One of the fund raising projects for the association was a scissor sale (the handy fold up kind).

3. One of the major issues during this year was the question of insurance coverage for psychiatric care.

1974*

President: Coralee (Corky) Muzzy

Vice President: Pauline Petterson

Secretary: Yvonne Johnson

Treasurer: Sue Milton

Delegate: Linda Johnson

Alternate Delegate: Judy Rowe

Major Events:

1. OTAO monthly meetings were split with the Certified Occupational Therapy Assistants meeting together and Occupational Therapists (OTR) meeting together.

2. The newsletter was chosen as the priority for the year at the annual meeting.

3. In October of this year the first manpower studies were completed regarding the need for the development of a four year (OTR) in occupational therapy in Oregon.

1975*

President: Grace Malpass

Vice President: Pauline Petterson

Secretary: Marian Reavley

Treasurer: Sue Milton

Delegate: Linda Johnson

Alternate Delegate: Judy Rowe

Major Events:

1. There were 134 members of OTAO.

2. The association looked into the possibility of obtaining non-profit status.

3. The emerging issues included peer review, licensure, legislation, reimbursement, and continuing education.

4. The executive board began to develop standard operating procedures (SOP) for each committee.

1976*

President: Susan C. Nelson

Vice President: Kay Rhoney

Secretary: Marian Neevel

Treasurer: Sue Milton

Representative: Linda Johnson

Alternate Representative: Judy Rowe

Major Events:

1. The major focus this year was the Licensure Bill (to be submitted to the 1977 Oregon legislature.)

2. The membership committee began the task of identifying all therapists in the state and arranging meetings around the state ("Getting to Know You".).

3. The job description of the vice president was changed. This position traditionally in the association was a program chairman position. It was changed to included more responsibility (assisting the president, etc.)

5. There were 170 members of OTAO (119 OTR's, 42 COTA's, and 9 others).

6. The annual conference of the American Occupational Therapy Association was held in San Francisco, California, October 11-15, 1976. The annual OTAO conference was held at the Child Development and Rehabilitation Center on May 21-23.

6
Licensure: 1977

Oregon State Capitol Building. Image credit: M.O. Stevens.

1977*

President: Susan C. Nelson

Vice President: Kay Rhoney

Secretary: Robin Sutton

Treasurer: Kai Galyen

Representative: Linda Johnson

Alternate Representative: Judy Rowe

Major Events:

1. Licensure was the issue of the year. On July 27, 1977, Governor Bob Straub signed the Occupational Therapy Practice Act.

3. The membership of OTAO continues to grow. There were 193 members this year.

4. The annual conference of the Occupational Therapy Association of Oregon was held May 21-23 at the Child Development and Rehabilitation Center.

HISTORICAL CONTEXT OF THE OREGON OT LICENSURE BILL

—Sue Nelson

In 1974 the legislative committee of the Occupational Therapy Association of Oregon began an initial study of the licensure issue. The primary purpose of licensure is to protect the client with standards of practice. It was my concern that the national trend seemed to be licensing professionals in order to develop and maintain standards of practice. If Oregon continued to be a non-licensing state, we would risk professional growth opportunities, lowered salaries, and possible mal-practice concerns for dissatisfied clients. At this time the American Occupational Therapy Association was against licensure. This was especially true of such important people in the association as Wilma West, a leading scholar and AOTA president at the time. The committee made a proposal to the executive board during the Spring 1975. It was felt by the committee that it was important to work on this issue as an association. At this time there was not a feeling of unity among the members of the association. This proposal was presented at the annual meeting in 1975. The decision was to proceed. A Licensure Steering Committee was appointed and they proceeded to interview four attorneys to assist with the project. Eventually, Kevin O'Connell was chosen to represent us. The beginning of 1976 was spent gathering information regarding the issue of licensure and presenting this information to Mr. O'Connell. At the annual membership meeting in May 1976, a decision was made to make the issue of licensure the priority of the state association. We were now on our way to seeking licensure in the state of Oregon.

Sue Nelson, president of OTAO in 1974, and Kay Rhoney, Vice President, spearheaded the licensure effort. Our efforts were greatly enhanced by a decision that came out of the December 1976 National Conference of Health Insurance. The decision from this conference to support the practice of occupational therapy was important in that the State Insurance Commissioner was one of our major testifiers. Prior to this encouraging development, the Oregon Health Division, a public health organization dedicated to empowering people through lifelong well-being, had refused to sponsor the bill.

The next step in the legislative process was to develop packets of information on occupational therapy to be delivered to each legislator prior to the legislative session. The Sessions began in January 1977 and the first reading of our bill was heard March 1, 1977. It was introduced to the Senate where it was assigned to the Labor, Consumer and Business Affairs Committee. The bill left that committee on May 11th and was sent to the Senate Ways and Means. At this point the economic impact issues were discussed and it was forwarded to the Senate Floor. The Senate passed the bill on June 21, with a vote of 23-6. At this time the bill was forwarded to the House. On June 22, 1977, it was assigned to the Rules Committee and the Ways and Means. This phase of the process came to be known as the period of the "Saturday Amendments". This was because of a hearing on a Saturday morning that was particularly "nerve wracking". Six amendments were proposed from this hearing, none of which passed. On July 3, 1977, the House passed the bill by a vote of 38-10. The Occupational Therapy Practice Act (Licensure Bill) was signed by Governor Bob Straub on July 27, 1977.

Approximately six months after the bill was signed, the members of the licensure board were appointed. The original board members were-

Keeston Lowery, OTR-President

Jean Ecklund, OTR

Kay Rhoney, OTR

Billie Willians-Consumer Member

William Bold-Consumer Member

This history was compiled as part of the packet of information delivered to all legislators prior to the legislative session of January 1977. Although the American Occupational Therapy Association was formed in 1917, it was not until 1946 that services of occupational therapists were provided in Oregon. The World War II medical facilities were mainly responsible for expanded services at that time. The first occupational therapy departments were organized at the Army facility in Vancouver and at the V.A. Hospital in Portland. Morningside Hospital was treating patients during the poliomyelitis epidemic and the occupational therapy department was organized to expand rehabilitation.

Occupational therapy departments began to provide services in other areas – Salem State Hospital and Rehabilitation Institute of Oregon (formerly the Portland Rehabilitation Center) in 1947, University of Oregon Medical School (1949), and Holladay Park Hospital (1950).

Occupational therapists began to organize to discuss mutual interests in 1948, and formed the Occupational Therapy Association of Oregon with twelve members in 1950. Currently in 1976, the association has 178 members (as recorded in 1976):

114 registered occupational therapists

38 certified occupational therapy assistants

26 aides and students

There are 71 occupational therapists in addition to the members of our association, making a total of 249 therapists working throughout the state of Oregon.

As recorded in 1976, there were approximately 230 registered occupational therapists and certified occupational therapy assistants residing in Oregon, their areas of service are as follows:

PHYSICAL DISABILITIES (hospitals, rehab centers, outpatient): 78

LONG TERM CARE FACILITIES (nursing homes, hospitals): 40

HANDICAPPED CHILDREN (CDRC, hospitals, schools): 24

PSYCHIATRIC (in/out patient, local/state/federal): 16

HOME HEALTH SERVICES (VNA, Associated Home Health): 10

GOODWILL, VOCATIONAL REHABILITATION: 4

MT HOOD COMMUNITY COLLEGE: 3

The following letter from Bill Casey was included in the original packet of information to legislators (1977) as an example of an occupational therapist seeing the need for licensure in practice. It acts as a specialized example of how licensure can help honor our specific skills within physical disability settings.

Members of the Committee:

My name is Bill Casey. I am a registered occupational therapist working presently at the Rehabilitation Institute of Oregon (RIO) – a 30-bed inpatient and outpatient unit which is a division of Good Samaritan Hospital and Medical Center in Portland, Oregon. Licensure of the occupational therapist is important to me because of many things; but, primarily it is important because I know the type of patients I work with don't need anybody other than knowledgeable health professionals.

Last year we at RIO saw 114 persons who have permanently lost the use of all or almost all of their limbs, and about 35 percent of these were under the age of 30. Each of these were also treated by occupational therapists. Most of these were victims of motor vehicle accidents within the state resulting in lesions of their spinal cord; and, as more sophisticated medical equipment and training becomes available for aiding these people to maintain vital body systems immediately following their injury, we at RIO expect to see more and more people surviving what were previously fatal accidents. The occupational therapist, if qualified, can help change survival into a meaningful and useful life for these people.

Likewise, last year we saw 88 cases of brain damage from around this and other states – the majority from car accidents as well as many others who required physical rehabilitation for diagnoses such as multiple sclerosis, stroke, amputations, cerebral palsy, and many other crippling causes. Medicine in its traditional form can not go very far in providing health again to these people. I feel these people do not need further advice from the many individuals who mis-name themselves "therapists", yet have nothing useful to offer the patient. On the other hand, if intervention by a licensed occupational therapist is made appropriately, permanent emotional and physical damage can be avoided.

Of the 45 occupational regulatory agencies now in existence, 13 are concerned with directly regulating the providers of health care in our state. The occupational therapist is presently only loosely defined as to role and function, almost totally unregulated legally, and yet is now employed in almost every major hospital in the state.

Many of the patients I treat two to three months after their injury have already had the proper splinting and physical treatment by occupational therapists. They are familiar with and motivated to continue the long, hard process towards living independently again. Others, usually because these services were not provided by the medical staff at a crucial time of I.V.'s, surgeries, etc. take longer to regain strength, movement, and ambition at RIO. There is no other replacement for a good occupational therapist. The bill you have before you is a good one and I feel its passage will insure the people of this state with protective measures to assure that they will have the services of a good occupational therapist.

Sincerely,

Bill Casey

To address the legislature, it is important to have legal consult to carry the bill. Legislators need specific information about the profession in order to understand how standards should be implemented. The below example displays how important it is to educate others and advocate for our profession's growth and development.

January 10, 1977

Members of the Oregon Legislature:

I'm writing on behalf of the Oregon Association of Occupational Therapists in connection with the licensure bill submitted to this session of the legislature. The bill provides for licensure of occupational therapists and occupational therapist assistants and sets standards and qualifications for these personnel.

A brief background of occupational therapy may familiarize you with the scope of the request and the reasons the Oregon association is seeking licensure.

The American Occupational Therapy Association was formed in 1917, although it was not until 1946 that services of occupational therapists were provided in Oregon. The World War II medical facilities were mainly responsible for expanded services at that time. The first occupational therapy departments were organized at the army facility in Vancouver and at the V.A. Hospital in Portland.

The occupational therapist provides health services for people of all ages in a wide variety of settings including; hospitals, nursing homes, health maintenance organizations, public heath centers, mental health centers, rehabilitation centers, schools, and facilities for the developmentally disabled, as well as private patient homes. Clients of occupational therapists include stroke patients, minimally blind, kidney dialysis patients, severely burned children and adult, accident victims who have lost arms or hands, and individuals with spinal cord injuries. Occupational therapy is also an essential part of the service provided in psychiatric mental health and mental retardation units.

Occupational therapists often work for the person who has been partially paralyzed or disable by a stroke, spinal cord injury, or arthritis. The therapist helps the patient learn how to compensate for loss of function in the affected limbs or extremities. They frequently design and fabricate adaptive equipment to improve the functioning of hands and arms. Improper positioning or untrained supervision in the use of this equipment can easily result in permanent damage for the patient.

It is also quite common for a child with severe burns or an adult who has had hand surgery to be referred to the occupational therapist by a plastic surgeon. The protection of these patients requires the experienced practitioner to be familiar with physiological, and psychological elements of these injuries. In the Portland area, the occupational therapist is an integral part of the care team of the Oregon Burn Center at Emanuel Hospital.

Occupational therapists also treat children with sensory and perceptual problems. Treatment by persons without appreciation of the complexities of such neurological defects and deficits may result in reinforcement of the problems.

For example, at the University of Oregon Health and Science Center, the occupational therapy department carries out two treatment programs, one for emotionally disturbed patients and the other program to service both in-patients and out-patients with physical disabilities. Within the psychiatric occupational therapy program the therapist evaluates and teaches activities of daily living (ADLs) which involves self-help skills, homemaking skills, as well as task oriented and social skills. Through a wide variety of activities (planning meals, field trips on buses, dancing, craft activities, self-care skills, volunteer jobs, etc.) the therapist is emphasizing the interpersonal relationship. The goal of guiding people to make maximum use of their potential and to develop new patterns of behavior remains the same although the method may vary. In the physical disabilities occupational therapy program the therapist evaluates patients with strokes, spinal cord injuries, rheumatoid arthritis, head injuries and treats them to increase their arms/hand function, in dependence of self-care and dependence of other activities of daily living such as cooking, cleaning, typing, etc. Patients with rheumatoid arthritis are most often seen as outpatients. The arthritic patient has a program that generally includes splinting from wrist to hand to decrease pain, postpone deformity and increase functional use and preparation of adaptive equipment such as a button hook to increase the ease of buttoning independently, and a car door opener to allow independent opening of the door without damaging joints.

These brief examples tend to illustrate the role the occupational therapist serves in some of the most significant and crucial areas of health care. This profession works primarily with individuals whom illness or injury have rendered him unable to perform satisfactorily the daily tasks of living.

Persons in these circumstances can be seriously harmed if proper safeguards are not maintained to ensure high quality care. Over the years, the Oregon association in connection with the American Occupational Therapy Association has attempted to protect the public and guarantee the integrity of the profession through the development and maintenance of standards of education, training, and practice. These standards underlie the certification process that the American Association attempts to require of anyone who seeks to practice occupational therapy. Many institutional and governmental providers recognize the certification standards of the national association.

Nevertheless, there have been instances in which unqualified personnel have attempted to provide vital services to an uninformed patient which has been detrimental. As you will note in the language of the bill, the educational standards for occupational therapy are high. The occupational therapist is required to have a baccalaureate degree in the field and the occupational therapy assistant must be a graduate of an approved program such as that at Mt. Hood Community College and also have field experiences.

The Oregon Association believes at present time that licensure will provide the most effective means for ensuring the protection of Oregon citizens who require occupational therapy treatment. Further, the statutory recognition may provide an impetus so that the under-treated and non-treated are referred now to licensed personnel. A law of this kind would make the profession legally accountable for the quality of health care that it delivers. This is a goal that has been sought by the Oregon Association for several years as is evidence by the outstanding continuing education programs it offers to occupational therapists, occupational therapy assistants, and occupational therapy aides and students throughout the state.

Nor is the potential exposure to under-trained, non-qualified personnel holding themselves out as occupational therapists, the only risk and detriment to the public which might be avoided by licensure. It should be noted that in this day of high health care costs and increasing involvement of federal governmental agencies, insurance coverage for the citizens of Oregon is a meaningful issue to be addressed. There have been instances where patients have suffered financially because certain insurance policies did not recognize the occupational therapist as a covered health care provider. Indeed, in Oregon there has been an instance where the state, as a third party insurer, has failed to provide coverage for occupational therapy. Those state agencies dealing with rehabilitation are great consumers of occupational therapy care and, as will be seen by supportive letters, much in favor of licensure for occupational therapists. The Welfare Division has, on occasion, refused payment for such services.

In an attempt to make health insurance acts uniform, the recently drafted model, Comprehensive Health Insurance and Health Care Cost Containment Act (prepared by the National Association of Insurance Commissioners) would not have specifically covered occupational therapy provided for patients. Through the assistance of knowledgeable commissioners such as Lester Rawls of Oregon, the model act has just been amended to put occupational therapists on par with their sister profession, physical therapy. Nevertheless, there are many insurance companies which will limit coverage to a licensed health care provider. Indeed, this is a trend encouraged by the federal government. For example, in recruiting occupational therapists for the Peace Corps it is noted that a condition of qualification is the obtaining of a bachelor's degree in occupational therapy and also licensure. While there are several east coast states which have licensure (New York, Georgia, and Florida) there are as yet only one-third of the states with bills for licensure before them. The bill presented to you is an attempt to protect the Oregon consumer, both in assuring and maintaining quality standards of service and fiscal responsibility through insurance coverage for this needed health care service. Your support for the passage of this legislation will be a meaningful endorsement for the many who will depend upon it in the future.

Attached to this presentation are letters of support from those people most knowledgeable with occupational therapy. No other health care providers feel threatened by the notion of licensure for occupational therapists. In fact, it is supported by other members of the teams since it is in their interest to be assured that patients are receiving care from highly trained professionals and that to the extent possible, cost of this care to the patient may be equitable borne by third party providers.

It should be pointed out that the potential for abuse in this area, while obviously not as great as an untrained person masquerading as a physician or dentists, does present a real threat upon the citizens of this state.

Very truly yours,

Kevin O'Connell, Attorney-at-Law

Pictured: Top Row (left to right): Bill Casey, Jim Nelson, Marion Merrick, Edna Ellen-Bell, Ruthanne Moore, *Unknown; Bottom Row (left to right): Linda Johnson, *Unknown, Kay Rhoney, Audrey Kerseg, Sue Nelson. Imaged provided by OTAO. Used with permission.

Pictured: OTAO members (left to right) Edna-Ellen Bell, Linda Johnson, Audrey Kerseg, Sue Nelson, Marion Merrick, and Kay Rhoney. & Gov. Staub. Image provided by OTAO. Used with permission.

The below articles were included in OTAO's newsletter, Viewpoint, as a way to help members understand the "behind the scenes" work of the Oregon OT Licensing Board. As of 2016, it has been 38 years since licensure was written into Oregon state law.

Viewpoint

Getting to Know Your Licensing Board: Meet Peggy Smith

You have read our series about the five Licensing Board members—the two public members, and the three OT members. And now you need to get acquainted with the person that really runs the ship! Meet Peggy Smith, our Executive Officer and office manager.

Peggy has an excellent foundation to her many skills, having graduated from Pfeiffer College in North Carolina with a BA in English and history, and was an English teacher in her first job. She joined the Gold Rush in 1961 and moved out to Oregon with her husband, Louis, to seek their fortunes.

Peggy came to our Board in 1981 with a wide variety of prior work experience. She was support staff to a construction company where her responsibilities included locating or replacing "lost" or damaged heavy equipment for naval construction in Vietnam (how can you lose large earthmovers and tractors?). She was general office assistant on a ranger station and predicted the weather (spit on your finger, hold it up to determine wind direction and divide by dew point—add visibility, etc.). She was lead secretary in the Health Division for Environmental Health and knows all about contaminated water supplies and "how to bury a relative in your backyard." And now she knows all things about occupational therapy and is never afraid to ask.

Peggy has been the biggest one-person fan club our profession has ever had in the state of Oregon. Her commitment to our board has been more than admirable, and that loyalty was honored when she received the Certificate of Apprecia-

Peggy Smith,
OT Licensing Board

tion from OTAO in 1988. If you ask her about it she will tell you she treasures that right on even par with her marriage license and her children's birth certificates.

Peggy and Louis, a newly retired civil engineer (Peggy assures me that she is not thinking of retiring) have two children: her son, Charlie, a newly graduated attorney, and Caroline, a past journalism student but now also a law student. Maybe they have both benefited from their mother's involvement in state government, justice and "apple pie"!

Peggy's interests include traveling, hiking, finding and restoring "junque," gardening, baking and political activities. If you ask her what special people have been a positive influence in her life, her answers might be: Therese Von for charity, Judi Beverly for enthusiasm, Kathy Hoffmann-Grotting for warmth, Karen Kennard for commitment, Cathy Vorhies for "quick study," Martin Friedman for perseverance, Charlotte Maloney for her unbiased review of issues, Kay Rhoney for her accomplishments in organizing the first board, Sue Nelson for her vision and professionalism, and especially Jean Van for her dedication and charity.

Now you know why we rely on Peggy to let us know "which way the wind blows" to guide us through these trying times. She's the best person in the world to help us move heaven and "earth" and in this next legislative session we may just need to do that.

We love you, Peggy.

*Sue Nelson,
Licensing Board Chair*

OTAO publication. Used with permission.

1992

Viewpoint

The OT Licensing Board: Who are They?

Recent articles in the *Viewpoint* have introduced you to members of the OT Licensing Board. Have you ever wondered why these particular individuals are on the Board? Are you wondering if you misplaced a ballot some time and forgot to vote for these people? Well, you didn't and the purpose of this article is to inform you about the process of selection and appointment to the OT Licensing Board.

The OT Licensing Board was created through state legislation in 1977 and is a state agency in the Health Division. This same legislation states:

• There will be five members on the Board, three of whom shall be licensed occupational therapists in this state with no less than three years of experience in OT immediately preceding their appointment, and two of whom shall be members of the consuming public.

• The term of office is four years and members may not serve more than two consecutive terms.

• OT Board members may be selected by the Governor from a list of no less than eight nominees submitted by OTAO.

The process goes something like this—months before a position for a professional position becomes available. Peggy Smith (OT Licensing Board Secretary) notifies the President of OTAO of the pending opening. Names are then generated, peoples c.v.'s are collected by OTAO and all of this goes to the Governor's Appointment Secretary. Time goes by and follow-up phone calls from the Governor's office begin to occur. The decision as to whom to appoint is the Governor's but the appointment is subject to Senate confirmation. This means that the OT selected must go before a committee comprised of 6-8 state senators and present a good impression and account of themself. This "confirmation hearing" lasts about 3rd minutes and the OT to be questioned has no doubt spent hour/days/weeks thinking about how it will go. Upon confirmation, another appointment is made for the official "swearing-in" with the Governor. This little ceremony lasts about 1½ minutes but nonetheless inspired this writer on several levels. First, it isn't every day that you go to meet with the Governor, just the two of you, albeit for 1½ minutes. Secondly, and more importantly, you realize that you have assumed responsibility for carrying out the licensing laws for the state of Oregon. If you didn't truly appreciate the seriousness or weight of this position before now somehow those 1½ minutes do it. It's official.

The consumer (sometimes called "public") members of the Board go through the same process only the names submitted to the Governor's appointment secretary come from many sources. The OT community has been involved in submitting names of persons for these positions, most often patients or family members of patients with whom the therapist has worked.

It seems appropriate here to tell you who the members of the Licensing Board are: Susan Nelson, OTR; Charlotte Maloney, OTR; Cathy Vorhies, OTR; Marti Friedman, Karen Kennard. Peggy Smith is executive secretary to the Board and manages the office, located in the state office building in Portland.

An issue which the OT Licensing Board addressed this past legislative session was the fact that the Board is limited in size to only five members. It takes legislation to increase the size of the Board and the Board introduced such a bill but it was unsuccessful—no surprise in the current political climate. However, in a profession as diverse in practice as OT it is very important that expertise in different areas of practice be represented on the Board. In addition, as the workload of the Board increases (there are now 869 licensed OTs), additional members would lighten the load all around. In the meantime, the five members currently serving on the Board offer their best to fulfill their charge, to monitor the practice of occupational therapy in Oregon.

Cathy Vorhies
OT Licensing
Board Member

The author being sworn into the OT Licensing Board by Governor Roberts.

OTAO publication. Used with permission.

7
Career Mobility: 1978-1990

Leadership Sketch, from OTAO publication. Artist Unknown. Used with permission.

1978*

President: Kay Rhoney

Vice President: Pat Theisen (Rosemary Kondrasuk after September)

Secretary: John Wirth

Treasurer: Kai Galyen

Representative: Judy Rowe

Alternate Representative: Marti Spicer

Senior Trustee: Kelly Tharp

Junior Trustee: Judy Meredith

Major Events:

1. The first licensure board was appointed: Keeston Lowery, OTR, President, Jean Ecklund, OTR, Kay Rhoney, OTR, Billie Williams, and William Bold. Glen Gee is executive secretary.

2. Continuing Education was voted as the number one priority by the membership at the annual conference (May 19-21).

3. The total membership of O.T.A.O. was 234 (158 OTR's, 42 COTA's, and 34 students).

5. The Josephine Moore Workshop was held February 17-19.

6. This was the first year of the trustee positions on the O.T.A.O. Executive Board (the purpose was to facilitate communication to members throughout the state).

OT Sketch from 1982, from OTAO Publication. © Mary Rutt, LPT. Used with permission.

The below information is included for reader's to understand the many efforts OT educators made to advance leaders in the profession. Oregon OTs understood the profession needed to move forward and this was their response to that need. Although successful, the program was short-lived due to low enrollment at the COTA school and the future development of an OTR career track (non-existent in Oregon until the mid 1980's).

INTRODUCTION TO THE CAREER MOBILITY PLAN

FOR THE CERTIFIED OCCUPATIONAL THERAPY ASSISTANT

September 1977

1. WHAT IS THE CAREER MOBILITY PLAN?

The Career Mobility Plan offers COTA's the opportunity for acquiring additional qualifications in order to practice as an Occupational Therapist, Registered, without returning to a formal academic setting. The plan recognizes that knowledge of and skills in occupational therapy can be developed through accumulated, related academic, clinical or practical experience in lieu of a formal educational program.

The program utilizes independent study and field work experience to enhance the COTA's knowledge and skills, so that the individual is prepared to function at the professional level of a registered occupational therapist. Our professional concern is to provide an opportunity for career advancement while at the same time, ensuring quality practice.

Individuals who meet established criteria (as described below), successfully pass the certification examination for OTR and pay the current certification fee will receive OTR credential and be eligible to practice as Occupational Therapist, Registered.

1. WHO QUALIFIES? WHAT ARE THE CRITERIA FOR COTA ENTRY TO THE CERTIFICATION EXAMINATION FOR OCCUPATIONAL THERAPIST, REGISTERED?

CRITERION 1: Current certification by AOTA as an occupational therapy assistant.

Explanation: The applicant must have paid the annual certification fee for current year at the time application to the Career Mobility

Plan initiated and must maintain active certification status through the time of admission to the examination.

CRITERION 2: Accumulation of not less than four (4) years of occupational therapy practice as a COTA; i.e. full-time or part-time equivalent of not less than four (4) years.

Explanation: 1) "four-years" – 48 months – confirmed by AOTA records and verified by employer.

2) "practice as a COTA" – COTA function delivering satisfactory direct client services under the supervision of an OTR as delineated in Occupational Therapy: Its Definition and Functions (Part II – Basic Entrance Level Qualifications, Roles and Functions) (see enclosures)

3) "full-time" – that equivalent to the regular work week as established by the employing facility.

4) "part-time" – that equivalent of no less than one-half of the work week, established by the employing facility, to be in consecutive work units of no less than six-month periods with an accumulation equal to four years of full-time work.

CRITERION 3: Evidence of having fulfilled current field work experience requirements,

stipulated in the Essential of an Accredited Educational Program for the Occupational

Therapists, 1973.

Explanation: 1) The minimal requirement is six (6) months of successfully completed, therapist-level field work experience as evaluated by the Career Mobility Review Committee.

2) Content of Field Work Experience (FEW): The FEW should be structured to fulfill the education needs of an entry-level

Occupational Therapist, Registered, since field work experience evaluations will be based on performance expectations of a beginning OTR. The FEW is expected to include clients/patients of both sexes, varying types of disabilities and levels of chronicity, all age ranges, and a variety of developmental stages. Experiences should also include a range of occupational therapy functions, e.g. prevention and health maintenance, remediation, daily life tasks and vocational adjustment, and pertinent types of communications such as case conferences, written reports, chart notes. The FEW should complement the applicant's previous experiences and acquired knowledge and skills. In other words, if an individual has worked for 4 years in a psychosocial setting, it would be advantageous to emphasize the area of physical dysfunction in their FEW.

3) It is the applicant's responsibility to make the preliminary arrangements for the FEW. The recommended procedure is for the candidate to first identify the types of learning experiences that would best enhance and complete their training, and then to investigate available resources (in compliance with guidelines listed below) for FEW in conjunction with these educational needs. ALL PLANS FOR FEW SHOULD REMAIN TENTATIVE UNTIL APPROVED BY THE REVIEW COMMITTEE.

4) Guidelines for Making Preliminary Arrangements For FEW:

1. The field work requirement must be a separately arranged experience, i.e. the requirement cannot be fulfilled as part of the 4 years work experience requirement.

2. The FEW must be arranged in a field work center which has an established program for the therapist-level student. This requirement can be waived by the Review Committee only if there is undue hardship for the candidate and if the evaluation of the candidate will not be jeopardized.

3. The FEW can be arranged in the present employment situation

if it is an established field work experience center and appropriate arrangements are made for release from COTA responsibilities during the FEW. It is recommended that the FEW Supervisor should not be the same person who has previously supervised the candidate as a COTA.

III. IS THE CAREER MOBILITY PLAN FOR YOU?

AOTA is proud of the Career Mobility Plan as an example of career laddering in the field of occupational therapy. As of April 1977, 34 individuals have achieved OTR credentials through this program and 40 are currently enrolled in the plan.

There are important considerations to be evaluated before embarking on this plan. There may be significant implications for this plan found in state licensure bills, civil service standards, and requirements of other potential employers. The consensus of opinion is that successful completion of the Career Mobility Plan requires substantial effort and time. Certainly the decision to make this kind of commitment is an important one. In considering the value of this program and your readiness for it in relation to your own career development, we hope you will find these guidelines for self-evaluation useful:

1. See Occupational Therapy: Its Definition and Functions, Part II.

(enclosure) Where would you see yourself in relation to function? The COTA eligible to apply for the Certificaiton Examination for Occupational Therapist, Registered, should be capable of functioning as an OTR as described, and should be able to demonstrate such ability.

2. Use the Performance Profile and Rater's Guide (see enclosures) to assess your knowledge and skill more specifically.

3. Have someone else evaluate you. Discuss your findings with

an experienced occupational therapist or have a separate assessment completed, using the same documents and compare the two. A frank discussion may produce a list of gaps in your knowledge and skills. Keep these assessments for your own use. Do not send them to AOTA.

4. Study your findings.

1. a) Consider which areas require further study and what resources you have available.

1. b) Begin to prepare a plan of independent study and evaluate its feasibility. The enclosure "How I Learn" provides another help in planning.

Study Guides listing references have been prepared by the Certification Committee. They are keyed to the Performance Profile and The Reference Handbook for Continuing Education in Occupational Therapy, 1970. See Statement of Intention (enclosure) for cost and how to order Study Guides. The Handbook is available from Kendall/Hunt Publishing Co., 2460 Kerper Blvd., Dubuque, Iowa 52001. $3.95

1. RECOMMENDED PROCUDERS FOR PARTICIPATION: (All material to be returned to AOTA should be sent to the Division of Certification)

1. Compete the Statement of Employment and/or Intention

2. a) If after your self-evaluation you decide "The Career Mobility Plan is not for me," return only the Statement of Intention. We hope the time you have taken for the assessment has provided you with helpful information about yourself and the profession.

3. b) If you wish to continue the process:

150. Complete the Statement of Intention and send this along with the $150.00 processing fee.

151. Complete and return to AOTA the Statement of Employment including the description of your employment experience. AOTA will send employment verification and evaluation forms to your employment supervisor.

2. Begin to investigate field work experience alternatives, keeping in mind the education needs you have identified to round out your knowledge and skills. Use the Preliminary Plans for Field Experience and Independent Study Form as a guideline and return the form to AOTA when completed. NOTE: The FEW plans specified on the form are PRELIMINARY and should not be finalized until authorized to do so by the AOTA Career Mobility Review Committee.

3. Develop your individual plan of independent study which should be implemented before entering into your FEW. Discuss this plan with your potential FWE supervisor and together develop a tentative timetable and list of subjects for study prior to beginning the field experience. It is the best interests of the candidate, the FWE supervisor, and the candidate's clients, if the candidate is thoroughly prepared to participate in a therapist-level FWE. Complete the appropriate section of Preliminary Plans for Field Work Experience and Independent Study Form.

4. Wait for recommendations and/or suggestions from the Review Committee before you finalize your FWE.

5. Take steps to carry out recommend plans after you have received feedback from the Review Committee. These recommendations might include:

   1. More independent study.

2. Notification that your preliminary FWE plans do not yet meet the requirements established by the Review Committee, and suggestions for modifying the plans so that they are in accordance with the Career Mobility Plan's criteria.

3. Notification that your preliminary FWE plans have been approved by the Review Committee. At this time, you should finalize your plans with your FWE supervisor, and inform the AOTA that you are carrying out arrangements made so that field work performance report forms may be sent to the FWE supervisor.

6. Complete the field work experience. Your supervisor will send an evaluation of your performance to the AOTA at the end of the experience. The Review Committee will study all documentation submitted and will notify you of their decisions and recommendations.

7. When all criteria have been met, you will be notified of your eligibility to take the Certification Examination for Occupational Therapist, Registered, and will be sent the form for admission to the examination. Additional information about the administration of the examination will be included. Complete the form and return the application fee as directed.

THE AMERICAN OCCUPATIONAL THERAPY ASSOCIATION, INC.

6000 Executive Blvd., Rockville, MD 20852

September 1977

SUPPLEMENTARY INFORMATION COTA CAREER MOBILITY PLAN

This information answers questions most frequently asked about the Career Mobility Plan. It will be helpful as you consider the feasibility of the plan and/or become involved in the procedure.

–The implementation of the Career Mobility Plan is the responsibility of a Review Committee which is a subcommittee of the Certification Committee. The AOTA National Office Certification Division provides staff liaison and implements the plan as directed by the Review Committee.

–At present the Review Committee is composed of five (5) members and an Administrative Assitant: an OTA Educator, a COTA, a Physical Disabilities Field Work Supervisor, a Psychiatry Field Work Supervisor, and an OT Educator Field Work Coordinator. The committee members come from varying geographic locations, and are budgeted to meet three times each year.

–The meetings of the Review Committee are determined by the dates of the examination. The following schedule has been found to best meet the needs for review of material to meet due dates: March, May, November

–The Review Committee is primarily engaged in the review of information about the applicant in reference to the established criteria. Experience indicates that such review may extend over a few years and the focus of the review may change. If early communication implies some misinterpretation by the applicant, a preliminary review may provide clarification and suggestions. An initial revdiew of a substantive nature occurs only when the Statement of Employment Form and Statement of Intention have been received from the applicant two (2) months prior to meeting dates March 1, and September 1) so that evaluations and information can be obtained from supervisors and are on hand at the time of the meeting. An initial review often results in recommendations for Field Work Experience. One or more ongoing reviews may be needed during planning and implementation of FEW. A final total review, including evaluations of recommended FEW is made to determine if all criteria have been met and documented prior to formal admission to the examination.

–The examination is given twice each year, on the last Saturday of January and June. All documentation required in relation to the criteria for admission to the examination must be received by the AOTA for final review by November 1 for the January examination and April 1 for the June examination. We regret that no exemptions can be made to these deadlines. This timing permits necessary communications with prospective applicants, processing of materials, committee review and correlation with testing service which administers the examination and computes the results.

–Deadlines need to be considered well in advance. The need to locate and make arrangements for field work experience may take some time. In addition, candidates will need to set aside a period of time for study prior to actually beginning such experience. This experience is intended to demonstrate to the supervisor that you have the background knowledge and can apply it in the work situation at the required level of performance. Only reinforcement and supplementary learning should be expected during the experience.

–In order for FEW to be meaningful, the supervisor selected should be skilled in: client/patient evaluation and assessment, in planning and integration of treatment, in departmental programming with allied professionals and should be knowledgeable and skilled in teaching methods, guidance and supervision. It is strongly suggested that arrangements for the supervised field experience be made at a center currently providing this for the professional student or under a therapist who has previously supervised such students. Field work experience is desirable on a full-time basis. If equivalent time is used, it should not be less than half days consecutively scheduled, equating the time required.

One method of meeting the FEW requirement is a three-month affiliation of a physical dysfunction type and a three-month affiliation of a psycho-social type. The range of experiences required can sometimes be encompassed in such arrangement.

Many educational programs require a third experience in order to meet requirements. The COTA's FEW will be evaluated for as much variety as seems reasonable and possible at the present time. It is important to remember that an expansion in function beyond that of the COTA must have been demonstrated. Supervised practical experience which was part of an occupational therapy assistant program was planned to evaluate your readiness for your first job as a COTA and is not applicable. The fieldwork experience required for this plan requires demonstration of function expected of an occupational therapist.

–All forms for evaluation of your performance or requests for verification of information needed will be sent to supervisors from the AOTA.

–When all criteria are met and you have been accepted for the examination, an application form to the examination will be sent to you with instructions. The current examination fee is $75.00 for each examination and you may take the examination as often as you wish.

The below letter was written by Kai Galyen, OTR, as a response to developing education for occupational therapists. Although controversial, the advancement of OT in Oregon was necessary for professional development.

To Whom It May Concern,

As you may have suspected, I have some pretty strong feelings concerning some of the Resolutions printed in the January edition of the O.T. newspaper; specifically, resolutions GG and HH. I wanted to sort out those feelings – to get away from being simply reactionary, before approaching you with my input. I needed some time to think through whether I was against the resolutions only because they may affect me personally, or if I really felt they would negatively affect the association as a whole.

My soul searching took me over some of the same territory I traveled when I initially considered applying to the Career Mobility Program. My basic roadblock was that I was opposed to entry criteria for any profession which did not include a baccalaureate. My reasoning, however, did not seem sound. I found a lot of my prejudice set in the foundation of my upbringing in a professional family. The old "you must have a degree to be successful" rang in my head. Also, the excitement, the stimulation, the recognition of university involvement greatly appealed to me. Tearing down the roadblocks was painful but something I had to accomplish before I could continue with an alternate life plan. I can appreciate how someone not facing this dilemma, especially one who has reached their goal through investment in conventional routes, would have difficulty accepting the outcome.

My task involved looking around me; recognizing individuals functioning in professional capacities without benefit of specific education, and reassessing my value system. It took exploration of our present credentialing methods and discussion with many therapists. Without fail, every therapist and student I talked with minimized their educational background and put great emphasis on what they had learned in the field. Admittedly, this may have been what they thought I wanted to hear. However, their descriptions of how they gained practical knowledge and competence were convincing.

In twelve years of working with health professionals, I have observed that competence is not necessarily guaranteed by a baccalaureate or higher degree. My experience has shown me that competence seems dependent on the desire and commitment of the therapist to provide quality service to their clients. Although this commitment is evident in most therapists I have observed, it seems, at the least, inadequate of the National Association to depend on the discretion of the individual therapist to practice competently. Seemingly, as it has been pointed out for years, we need to develop a certification exam and ongoing certification methods that assure the competency of practicing therapists! And this is my conclusion. If the certification method truly measures competence, why should it matter how an individual acquires the skill to pass it?

Resolution GG states three concerns expressed by A.O.T.A. members, to which I would like to respond.

"1. Reliable data relative to performance are non existent for the 43 C.O.T.A.s who have been credentialed via this method."

Aside from my response to this concern, referral to these O.T.R.s as C.O.T.A.s arouses my anger. To do so because they lack a baccalaureate degree is either unthinking elitism, or deliberate snobbery.

In response to the first concern: It is true, "reliable data relative to performance is non existent" for the O.T.R.s credentialed in this manner. Isn't that why Resolution 518-77 (to study entry methods) was adopted? Don't we need reliable data relative to performance for all practicing therapists? I submit that this valid concern could be better met by establishing ongoing certification methods that measured competence of all therapists, rather than by limiting methods of entry.

"2. Other professions may view O.T. as technicians if credentialing via this method is continued."

Other professions may view O.T. as technicians if credentialing via this method is discontinued, as long as O.T.R.s cling to their technical skills. Measuring R.O.M., fabricating splints, and administering standardized tests are only a few examples of purely technical skills O.T.R.s continue to call their own. O.T.A. students are presently learning these skills in their classes, and are qualified to use them. O.T.R.s need to use their planning, interpretive, and administrative skills, and separate themselves from the technical tasks that can be performed with guidance by less educated personnel.

In our present nation wide struggle to be recognized as a unique health service, I doubt very much that other professionals are concerned with how 43 people got there. It seems rather, their interest would be focused on what all of you have to offer.

I certainly don't mean this personally but I submit that this concern could be better met by O.T.R.s presenting themselves and their tasks as professional, and divorcing themselves from those that are not. A concerted P.R. effort seems more appropriate than eliminating a method of entry which allows well-qualified therapists to join your professional ranks. And again, an ongoing certification method that assured competency could address this concern also.

"3. That the concept of upward mobility by equivalency examination does not recognize the contribution and value of education in the preparation of a professional."

I find it difficult to believe that whoever wrote that understood the process of Career Mobility. To be qualified for the program, the candidate must first have been certified as an O.T.A. Many O.T.R.s who have been practicing 10-15 years tell me that what C.O.T.A.s are getting in school now is far superior to what they received in their B.S. programs. Secondly, the candidate must have successfully completed a minimum of four years practice. They must submit a statement of employment describing the types of patient programs and other O.T. functions they were involved with at each facility they may have worked since O.T.A. graduation. Their supervisor(s) must submit a performance profile, evaluating them at "the minimal level of performance expected of a newly graduated O.T." [from "Performance Profile for COTA's Preparing For The Certification Examination"] So you see, the Career Mobility candidate must function at the level of a newly graduated O.T. before they even begin their challenge. This is when the education really begins.

They must call on every resource they can find, which may include students from several different O.T. programs, established O.T. practitioners and other health care professionals to suggest texts/speakers/papers/A.J.O.T. articles/courses – anything that might help them gain further knowledge. They must define their own weaknesses and find their own means to strengthen their background. They must form an Independent Study Plan, and arrange their own Field Work Experiences. All this information (Statements of Employment, Performance Profiles, Independent Plans, and arranged F.W.E.) must be submitted for review to the Certification committee. This group consists of an O.T.A. educator, a C.O.T.A., a Physical Disabilities Field Work Supervisor, and Psychiatry Field Work Supervisor, an O.T. Educator Field Work Coordinator, and an administrative assistant from A.O.T.A. As the candidate begins to study the materials they have gathered, the certification committee reviews their plan. This review may take several years and result in suggestions for additional or changed Independent Study of F.W.E. When they have finally completed their study and clinicals, "final total review, including evaluations of recommended F.W.E. is made to determine if all criteria have been met and documented prior to formal admission to the examination." [from Supplementary Information – COTA Career Mobility Plan] And then of course, they must pass the Certification Examination.

That is a commitment of at least eight years study and experience; one that may far exceed that of the baccalaureate student. I fail to see how that could possibly be construed as not recognizing the value and contribution of education. The candidate not only earns a valid O.T. education but, it seems to me, they gain far more in the areas of goal-directedness, long-range planning, and dealing with frustrations than the B.S. student. They are not only educated in one of the most stringent programs available, they must design their own curriculum to meet the criteria set by A.O.T.A. Perhaps with their skill level and experience, we should be calling on these 43 to help develop O.T. education programs, rather than degrading their entry route and doggedly continuing to refer to them as "C.O.T.A.s".

Concerning both Resolution GG and HH, I feel the association would be better off to await the results of Resolution 519-77. If flaws are found in any entry method that cannot be resolved, then of course that method should be abolished. In the meantime, it seems unfairly detrimental to the success of the program to disband it, even temporarily. Shouldn't we be using our energy in positive endeavors such as, mentioned before – developing the means to measure competency for all practicing therapists?

When you vote on these Resolutions in April, I hope you will consider these points. I urge you to vote "no" on Resolutions GG and HH, thus preserving an entry route into our chosen profession that can be of great benefit to the applicant and to the association as a whole.

Sincerely,

Kai Galyen, OTR

1979*

President: Kay Rhoney

Vice President: Cathy Vorhies

Secretary: Debbie Rice (also Shirley Elings)

Treasurer: Jolene Heitmann

Representative: Judy Rowe

Alternate Representative: Marti Spicer

Trustee: Judy Meredith

Junior Trustee: Marta Toynbee-Bogrand

Major Events:

1. Public Relations was voted as the number one priority by the membership at the annual conference May 18-19.

2. The Joy Huss workshop was held September 15-16.

4. The effort to meet with members throughout the state continued. This has been a long standing issue – that therapists who do not reside in the Portland area feel "isolated" because most events occur there.

5. A renewed effort was started to look into the possibility of developing a school of occupational therapy in Oregon. Pacific University is currently looking into this possibility with the target date for development set for 1983.

The following 7 photographs are conference materials from 63rd Annual AOTA Conference held in Portland, Oregon. They are included here to provide a specific example of the conference happenings, meetings, and special events.

AOTA publication. Used with permission.

Message from the Executive Director

James J. Garibaldi
Executive Director

The theme for the 1983 Annual Conference, "Balancing Environment and Individual," is particularly relevant as we look at the changing environment in which occupational therapists and other providers of health care now find themselves.

The passage of the Reconciliation Act in June of 1981 was a major change in the way our federal government conducts its legislative business. It also signaled a retrenchment in direct federal support of health and human service programs and a transfer of the responsibilities for the conduct of these programs to state and local governments.

This trend toward decentralization places a heavier financial burden on state and local governments and on the private sector. Given the state of our economy, these sources are finding it increasingly more difficult to meet the costs of providing services to a broad spectrum of recipients at a level of service considered appropriate and desirable.

Congressional action in 1982 has introduced a new dimension in payment for health care. The cost-per-case management concept in Medicare and its attendant features of prospective payment, incentive payments for cost reductions, and replacement of routine per diem cost limits with total operating cost-per-case limits ushers in computer technology to the management of health care.

This environment of cost containment is pervasive throughout every aspect of the health-care system. Searching questions are being asked about the need and cost effectiveness of treatment. More and more providers of health care are being asked to justify their services and to document their productivity. Utilization review and quality assurance are essential components of the new system.

The program planned for the 1983 Annual Conference addresses these issues and more, providing in-depth information and facts to help in everyday practice and to plan for the future. The special events provide an array of social activities and camaraderie. Throw in the spectacular scenery of the Northwest, the marvelous hospitality of the Oregonians, and the 1983 Annual Conference is something you can't miss.

Many, many thanks to the hundreds of people who have labored so long and hard to provide a conference agenda so finely tuned to current and future needs in the changing environment.

Message from the President

Carolyn Baum
President

I welcome you to join your professional colleagues at the 1983 Annual Occupational Therapy Conference in Portland, Oregon. The topic, "Balancing Environment and Individual," will encourage us to explore our important role in health care and, in addition, the roles and responsibilities of the consumers of health care — our patients.

Health care is undergoing some dramatic changes as costs, as well as technical advances, continue to soar. As a profession, and as individuals, we must have the knowledge of the health environment and the knowledge of our field to be effective and continue to grow.

The conference offers an important time for sharing, for reflecting, and for challenging us — all characteristics that lead to creating a balance for us as individual occupational therapists.

I hope you will join me and your colleagues for this important conference. The political, social, economic, and technological environment demands our attention. Only when we have a sense of our responsibilities and know we can have an impact can we be effective for our patients, for our facilities, for our profession, and for ourselves.

AOTA publication Used with permission.

AOTA Special Meetings and Events Schedule

Tuesday, April 12
9:00 AM– 6:00 PM
Commission On Practice
9:00 AM– 6:00 PM
Bylaws, Policies, Procedures Meeting

Wednesday, April 13
9:00 AM– 6:00 PM
Commission on Practice
9:00 AM– 5:00 PM
Executive Board
9:00 AM– 3:00 PM
ASCOTA Steering Committee —
Portland Marriott
9:00 AM– 9:00 PM
Standards and Ethics Commission
8:00 PM–10:00 PM
CSAP Orientation

Thursday, April 14
9:00 AM– 5:00 PM
Commission on Practice
8:30 AM– 5:00 PM, 7:00 PM–10:00 PM
CSAP Meeting
8:30 AM– 2:00 PM
Standards and Ethics Commission
9:00 AM– 2:30 PM
Executive Board
9:00 AM– 5:00 PM
Written History Committee of AOTA
3:00 PM–10:00 PM
Representative Assembly

Friday, April 15
8:00 AM–10:00 PM
Representative Assembly
8:30 AM– 5:00 PM
CSAP Management Workshop
8:30 AM– 9:30 PM
Accreditation Committee
9:00 AM– 5:00 PM
Written History Committee of AOTA
4:00 PM– 7:00 PM
Commission on Education —
Portland Marriott
7:00 PM– 9:00 PM
AOTF Membership — CSAP
9:00 PM–10:00 PM
RA/CSAP Reception

Saturday, April 16
8:00 AM–10:00 PM
Representative Assembly
8:30 AM– 5:00 PM
CSAP Task Groups and
Business Meeting
8:30 AM– 9:00 PM
Program Advisory Committee of COE
— Portland Marriott
8:30 AM– 9:30 PM
Accreditation Committee
12:00 NOON– 5:00 PM
Commission on Education —
Portland Marriott
4:00 PM– 9:00 PM
ASCOTA — Portland Marriott

Sunday, April 17
8:00 AM–10:00 PM
Representative Assembly
8:30 AM– 5:00 PM
Program Advisory Committee of COE
— Portland Marriott
9:00 AM–10:00 PM
Commission on Education —
Portland Marriott
9:00 AM– 5:00 PM
ASCOTA Delegate Meeting —
Portland Marriott
9:00 AM– 5:00 PM
Accreditation Committee
9:00 AM– 5:00 PM
Certification Committee
5:30 PM– 9:30 PM
Research Advisory Council

Monday, April 18
9:00 AM– 5:00 PM
ASCOTA Business Meeting —
Portland Marriott
9:00 AM– 5:30 PM
Commission on Education —
Portland Marriott
9:00 AM–12:00 NOON
Accreditation Committee
9:00 AM– 5:00 PM
Special Interest Section Steering
Committee
9:00 AM– 5:00 PM
Program Advisory Committee of COE
— Portland Marriott
1:00 PM– 5:00 PM
Certification Committee

Special Events
7:00 PM
Opening Ceremony
7:30 PM
Keynote Address
8:00 PM–10:00 PM
Student Mixer
8:30 PM
AOTF Auction

Tuesday, April 19
Special Events
8:45 AM– 9:30 AM
General Session — Wilma West
9:00 AM– 5:00 PM
Media Festival
9:30 AM
Exhibit Opening
9:30 AM– 1:30 PM
Roundtable — Roster of Fellows
and Roster of Honor
12 NOON
International Luncheon
2:30 PM
Eleanor Clarke Slagle Lectureship
3:00 PM– 5:00 PM
Student Mixer
6:30 PM
Soapbox II
8:00 PM
Awards Ceremony
9:15 PM
Awards Reception

Special Meetings
9:00 AM– 5:00 PM
AOTPAC Board Meeting
3:00 PM
Student Forum and Orientation
3:00 PM– 5:00 PM
AJOT Editorial Board
4:00 PM– 6:00 PM
Developmental Disabilities
Special Interest Section
4:00 PM– 6:00 PM
Gerontology Special Interest Section
4:00 PM– 6:00 PM
Mental Health Special
Interest Section
4:00 PM– 6:00 PM
Physical Disabilities Special
Interest Section
4:00 PM– 6:00 PM
Sensory Integration Special
Interest Section
4:00 PM– 6:00 PM
Administration Meeting
4:00 PM– 6:00 PM
Vocational Rehabilitation Meeting
4:00 PM– 6:00 PM
Licensure Board
6:30 PM– 9:30 PM
Black OT Caucus

Updated daily Meetings and Events Schedules will be available on-site during Conference

AOTA publication. Used with permission.

Wednesday, April 20
Special Events

7:30 AM
  Special Interest Section Breakfast
8:45 AM– 9:30 AM
  General Session — Shirley Zurchauer
9:00 AM– 5:00 PM
  Media Festival
9:30 AM
  Exhibits
9:30 AM– 1:30 PM
  Roundtable — Roster of Fellows and Roster of Honor
4:30 PM
  President's Open House
2:00 PM– 4:00 PM
  Annual Business Meeting
8:00 PM–10:00 PM
  AOTPAC Variety Show

Special Meetings

9:00 AM– 5:00 PM
  ASCOTA Steering Committee
9:00 AM– 1:00 PM
  Communications Committee
9:45 AM–11:30 AM
  AOTA International Committee
4:30 PM– 7:00 PM
  Research Forum
4:30 PM– 6:00 PM
  COTA Forum
4:30 PM– 6:00 PM
  Student Presentations
7:00 PM– 9:00 PM
  Male Advocacy Group

Special Events — Students

Saturday, April 16:
4:00 PM– 6:00 PM
  Student Orientation
7:00 PM– 9:00 PM
  Student Exchange

Monday, April 18:
8:00 PM–10:00 PM
  Student Mixer

Tuesday, April 19:
3:00 PM– 5:00 PM
  Student Forum
5:00 PM– 5:45 PM
  Student Orientation (repeat)

Thursday, April 21:
7:00 PM–10:00 PM
  AOTA Banquet

Thursday, April 21
Special Events

7:00 AM
  Fun Run
7:30 AM
  AOTF Breakfast
8:45 AM– 9:30 AM
  General Session — Janice Burke
9:00 AM– 5:00 PM
  Media Festival
9:30 AM
  Exhibits
9:30 AM– 3:30 PM
  Roundtable — Roster of Fellows and Roster of Honor
3:30 PM
  Treasure Chest Drawing
4:00 PM– 5:00 PM
  Inaugural Address
5:30 PM– 6:30 PM
  Fellows Reception
7:00 PM
  Annual Banquet

Special Meetings

9:00 AM– 3:00 PM
  ASCOTA Steering Committee
9:30 AM– 3:00 PM
  Poster Sessions
9:30 AM–12:00 NOON
  Executive Board

CSAP Schedule

Wednesday, April 13:
8:00 PM–10:00 PM
  CSAP Orientation (optional)

Thursday, April 14:
8:30 AM– 5:00 PM
  CSAP Meeting
7:00 PM–10:00 PM
  CSAP Meeting

Friday, April 15:
8:30 AM– 5:00 PM
  CSAP Management Workshop
7:00 PM– 9:00 PM
  AOTF Membership Meeting — CSAP
9:00 PM–10:00 PM
  RA/CSAP Reception

Saturday, April 16:
8:30 AM–12:00 NOON
  CSAP Task Groups
1:00 PM– 5:00 PM
  CSAP Business Meeting

Friday, April 22
Special Events

8:30 AM– 5:00 PM
  CSAP Management Workshop
2:30 PM– 3:30 PM
  Closing Session — Lela A. Llorens

Special Meetings

9:00 AM– 5:30 PM
  U.S. Army Occupational Therapy Meeting
9:30 AM–12:00 NOON
  Executive Board

ASCOTA Schedule

Wednesday, April 13:
9:00 AM– 3:00 PM
  ASCOTA Steering Committee

Saturday, April 16:
3:00 PM– 4:00 PM
  New ASCOTA Directors Orientation
4:00 PM– 6:00 PM
  Student Orientation
7:00 PM– 9:00 PM
  Student Exchange

Sunday, April 17:
9:00 AM– 5:00 PM
  ASCOTA Delegate Meeting

Monday, April 18:
9:00 AM–12:00 NOON
  ASCOTA Business Meeting
1:00 PM– 5:00 PM
  ASCOTA Task Force Meetings
8:00 PM–10:00 PM
  Student Mixer

Tuesday, April 19:
3:00 PM– 5:00 PM
  Student Forum
5:00 PM– 5:45 PM
  Student Orientation (repeat)

Wednesday, April 20:
9:00 AM– 5:00 PM
  ASCOTA Steering Committee (Old & New Directors)

Thursday, April 21:
9:00 AM– 3:00 PM
  ASCOTA Steering Committee (Old & New Directors)
7:00 PM–10:00 PM
  AOTA Banquet

AOTA publication. Used with permission.

Special Events

Monday, April 18

6:45 PM Opening Ceremony
View the sights of Oregon; its environment and the individuals who interact with its array of natural splendor through a slide and tape presentation when our opening ceremony begins. Hear the songs of celebration and fanfare as the Joyful Noise Vocal Arts Ensemble lead the processional of banners and dignitaries to be seated at the platform.

7:30 PM Keynote Address

8:30 PM AOTF Auction
Going . . . Going . . . Gone!!! Plenty of enthusiasm and plenty of excitement will greet bidders as they attend the Foundation's second Conference Auction. A whole selection of arts, crafts, antiques, novelty creations and contributions made and donated by occupational therapists will be offered for sale. Opening bids will begin 25-30% below market value. Come and enjoy a "tax deductible" evening with the Foundation and their "celebrity" auctioneers! (Your $5 ticket includes a cocktail.)

8:30 PM Student Mixer
An evening of fun and participatory entertainment . . . designed to give you the time of your life . . . meet students from all over the USA . . . refreshments served. Tickets: $2.00

Tuesday, April 19

9:30 AM Exhibit Opening
Commercial exhibitors will be displaying the newest products pertinent to occupational therapy. Take time to visit all the exciting displays Tuesday through Thursday.

9:30 AM Roundtable Discussions with Members of the Roster of Fellows and Roster of Honor
Roundtable discussions are scheduled at one-hour intervals throughout conference week to give you an opportunity to consult with your colleagues who are Members of the Roster of Fellows and Members of the Roster of Honor. These sessions are designed to stimulate discussion between Conference participants and esteemed members of the profession concerning specific issues affecting the profession.

10:00 AM–2:00 PM Want to Meet the New Associate Executive Directors of AOTA?
AOTA's three Associate Executive Directors will be available by appointment to discuss issues within their respective purviews: Madelaine Gray, Professional Services; Fran Acquaviva, Membership Services and Association Development; Bill Graves, Business and Finance.

10:30 AM OT Media Festival
See Audiovisual presentations developed by and for occupational therapists and the latest presentations available from AOTA. See your Daily Bulletin for times and titles of individual presentations.

12:00 NOON International Luncheon
Come join your colleagues for lunch. Guest speaker will be David Lawrence, M.D., Area Medical Director and Vice-President of Medical Operations, Northwest Permanente, P.C., Kaiser-Permanente Medical Care Program, Portland, Oregon. He will speak on the "Economics of Health Care: The Role of Industrialized Countries in Contributing to Health Care of Developing Nations."

2:30 PM Eleanor Clarke Slagle Lectureship
This year's lecturer will be Joan Rogers, Ph.D., OTR, FAOTA.

4:00 PM SIS Annual Business Meetings
All of the Special Interest Sections will hold business meetings. Check the program on Tuesday for each meeting's agenda.

6:30 PM Soap Box II
Members of the Roster of Fellows and Roster of Honor will have five minutes to expound on any controversial, thought-provoking, perhaps shocking ideas they have concerning occupational therapy and the health care community. There will be a cash bar, and people may mill around and challenge the members after their presentation.

8:00 PM Awards Ceremony
Join the Association in its annual recognition of the accomplishments of our outstanding professionals.

9:15 PM Awards Reception
You are invited to meet and greet the 1983 award recipients and listen to the harmonious melodies of the Stradivari Strings Ensemble during the Wine and Cheese Reception.

The Stradivari Strings will entertain during the Awards Reception.

AOTA publication. Used with permission.

Wednesday, April 20

7:30 AM **Special Interest Section Breakfast**
The Fifth Annual SIS Breakfast will feature Susan Fine as the guest speaker.

9:30 AM **Exhibit Viewing**

9:30 AM **Roundtable Discussion with Roster of Fellows and Roster of Honor**

10:30 AM **OT Media Festival**

2:00 PM **Annual Business Meeting**
Presidential Address
Carolyn M. Baum will reflect her thoughts with you on her presidency this past year.

8:00 PM **AOTPAC Variety Show**
The 3rd Annual AOTPAC Variety Show promises to be an enjoyable evening of singing, dancing, joking and more. The AOTPAC Board cordially invites you to see some of your colleagues display their numerous and varied talents. It will be a good time for all, so let your hair down and be there on Wednesday, April 20, at 8:00 PM. For only $5.00 you can have an evening of entertainment while supporting the American Occupational Therapy Political Action Committee.

Wholly Cats will appear at the Annual Banquet.

Thursday, April 21

7:00 AM **Fun Run**
Keep in shape during the convention by entering this 3-mile loop run through Portland's most beautiful park. The race will be timed for those of you with a competitive spirit though others may want to take time to enjoy the scenic views looking down at the city. Bus transportation will be provided between the Hilton and Washington Park. Prizes will be awarded and souvenirs for all.

7:30 AM **"Research: Zero to Five Years" — AOTF Breakfast**
It has been five years since the AOTF launched its new efforts in Research. Come see how the Foundation's Research Program has grown and what its plans are for the future. Guest speaker will be Ann Grady, OTR, FAOTA.

9:30 AM **Exhibit Viewing**

9:30 AM **Roundtable Discussion with Roster of Fellows and Roster of Honor**

9:30 AM **Poster Sessions**
Poster Sessions are scheduled during exhibit hours. Drop by to discuss the newest developments in the profession with the poster presenters. Check the program for Thursday for general titles and times.

10:30 AM **Media Festival**

4:00 PM **Inaugural Address**
The title of the address is "Beliefs in the New Beginning," and it will be presented by Robert K. Bing.

5:30 PM **Fellows and ROH Reception**
Distinguished members of the Roster of Fellows and Roster of Honor of the Association will sponsor a reception before the Annual Banquet to honor the new members added to the Rosters for 1983. Only FAOTAs and ROHs may attend this event.

6:30 PM **Cash Bar**

7:30 PM **Annual Banquet — Columbia River "GORGE" Night**
Swing and dine at the Red Lion Hotel to the sounds of the Wholly Cats during your Northwest "salmon bake" feast. After dinner, foot stomp to the music of the Metropolitan Jug Band and swing your partners to the calling of the Funlovers Square Dance Club of Portland. No single physical feature has influenced the development of the Pacific Northwest more than that of the Columbia River. Transportation is included in the cost of your dinner so you can explore the great, majestic river of the Northwest as you travel down its channel viewing its sparkling waters, city bridges, and the night lights of the City of Portland.

See the Metropolitan Jug Band at the Columbia River "GORGE" Banquet.

AOTA publication. Used with permission.

THE AMERICAN OCCUPATIONAL THERAPY ASSOCIATION
Annual Conference — April 18-22, 1983
Portland, Oregon

Local Committee

CHAIR
Debi Brunkow

ASSISTANT CHAIR
Lilian Crawford

SECRETARY
Shirley Elings

TREASURER
Marcia Postma

PROGRAM
Kathy-Hoffmann-Grotting

HOSPITALITY
Pauline Petterson

MANPOWER
Kay Bhoney
Colleen Thomas

STUDENT ADVISOR
Sherry Dickens

STUDENT COMMITTEE
Karla Oviatt
Terri Suhr-Neil

SCIENTIFIC EXHIBITS
John Wirth

ARTWORK AND PRINTING
Ina Rae Ussack

DAILY BULLETIN
Judi Beverly-Hinshaw

PUBLIC RELATIONS
Cathy Vorhies

SPECIAL EVENTS
Karen S. Foley

National Office Staff Liaisons

Executive Director
James J. Garibaldi

Associate Executive Director
Financial and Business Administration
William J. Graves

Director of Continuing Education
Martha M. Kirkland, OTR

Director of Public Affairs
Betty Cox, COTA, ROH

Conference and Meetings Director
Mardy Phillips

Assistant to Conference and
  Meetings Director
Beth Caudill

CHAIR AND ASSISTANT CHAIR
FINAL REPORT
1983 AOTA ANNUAL CONFERENCE

Chair: Debi Brunkow
Assistant Chair: Lilian Crawford

As Chair and assistant Chair of the Portland Local Conference Committee, we feel proud of the 63rd Annual AOTA Conference and would like to share some thoughts, general and specific, that we feel would be helpful in planning future Conferences.

It is difficult to imagine a more rewarding professional and personal experience. Indeed, we feel extremely thankful to have been a part of the Conference and to have had the opportunity to work with AOTA Staff so closely.

AOTA Publication. Used with permission.

The below document analyzes OTAO's involvement in the 1983 AOTA National Conference. Tireless efforts from many OTAO members created a very memorable event that is still talked about today. Perhaps this information could serve as a nice foundation for when the conference returns to Oregon in the future.

1983 AOTA Annual Conference

Final Report

Chair and Assistant Chair

Our Roles: It appeared important from the start to set the tone for the Committee and thus the Conference in the choice of Chair people. A balance of Certified Occupational Therapy Assistants and Occupational Therapists, Registered, "Good 'Ol Girls" and relative newcomers, in a wide range of personality styles help the Committee to function optimally. The Chairs were "workers" as well as idea generators and had high expectations of their performance. They were also people with multiple resources and generally positive, high energy people who were accepting of AOTA Staff decisions as they were not competing, simply supporting.

The Chair acted as a liaison between the Local Conference Committee and AOTA and constantly maintains an overall picture of Conference. With the position comes a fair amount of control and ultimately responsibility for all Committee work. It is essential to be organized.

The Assistant Chair ated as the balance to the Committee performing perception checks, interjecting humor and generally was willing to take on any task or attend to any committee. She functioned as an independent partner to the chair, frequently attending to special "people-oriented" recognitions which continually maintained Committee spirit. It was important that Mardy Phillips got to know both of us, both as individuals and as team members.

Timelines

August 1981: We definitely got off to a good start by having an attractive logo and appealing theme. We feel that this significantly contributed to the success of our Conference.

June 1982: This was the month for our kick off brunch and first "in-person" visit by Mardy. This made the up and coming Conference seem real. We carefully chose the setting for the brunch which coincided with ACPAC Meeting in Portland to excite and impress AOTA with the flavor of the city.

August 1982: Local Conference Committee picture was taken with consideration of environment and dress that is reflective of what we wanted to represent. Monthly meeting schedule is detail were set. Committee began to decide how it would function, leadership roles and styles, and generally how communication could be facilitated between Committee Chairs and between the Local Conference Committee and AOTA Staff.

Fall 1982: Details of the Local Conference Committee actions can be found in the minutes. Debi kept a running list of questions from the Local Conference Committee and spoke with Mardy every two to three weeks. Mardy relayed new tasks and questions that were then taken care of by the Local Conference Committee. It is important during this time for committees to get members and yet we had to keep a cap on the energy and enthusiasm so as to be careful not to gear up too soon. It seemed to be a particular trait of our Local Conference Committee Chairs to want to be well prepared far in advance and to get as many tasks as possible taken care of as soon as possible.

Note: Although Local Conference Committee met monthly beginning in August of 1982, we were able to take December off and keep activities at a minimum until January of 1983.

Winter 1982: Mardy's visit to Portland and individual meetings with

Local Conference Committee Chairs suddenly made the conference seem real and helped each committee focus on important tasks and where their emphasis should be placed. Enthusiasm continued to build.

Conference: It could not be emphasized enough that you must be prepared for anything and everything. On recommendation of the Philadelphia Local Conference Committee, we met each morning at 7:30 in the Hospitality Room to coordinate our day. This was extremely helpful early in the week but by Thursday, we no longer felt the need to meet. It seemed to work well for each of us, Chair and Assistant Chair, to tour through the hotel checking in with each Local Conference Committee Chair to problem solve, offer encouragement, run an errand, answer questions or simply troubleshoot. This "cruising" kept us visible and increased our awareness of what was happening in all areas. The Local Conference Committee seemed to congregate in their hotel suite, a convenient place to leave messages for one another and take brief time-outs.

Communication with AOTA staff: One of the greatest benefits of being a Local Conference Committee member was the opportunity to meet and work with AOTA staff. While it is said many times and in many ways, once again we need to emphasize the superior skills, guidance and expertise of Mardy Phillips. Remember that she is your best resource and keep communication open and honest. Our Local Conference Committee managed well in spite of not always agreeing with AOTA staff because we understood from the start that our input was important but final decisions would be made by AOTA.

Points to reinforce committee reports: We feel extremely proud of the Committee reports generated by our Local Conference Committee Chairs and would encourage each of the Kansas City Conference people to read them in detail. The following are just highlights which we personally felt we wanted to emphasize.

Secretary: We were able to cut secretarial costs by using resources within our committee for free Xeroxing and mailing. We would reinforce the recommendation given by the Secretary to combine the Secretary's job with either the Treasurer or Scientific Exhibits.

Treasurer: Combining the position of Secretary and Treasurer is another recommendation as neither has specific or time-absorbing task during Conference Week. We, as a Committee, came out under budget because of the resources each Committee Chair had available to them. While we are proud of that fact, we also understand that not every committee is able to pull the resources that he had.

Special Events: The Special Events Committee Report lacked narrative to let you know what an incredible amount of time and energy went into this Committee. It helps to have a high energy and performance Chair as well as a Committee with multiple and varied community resources. Each time money was spent, it had to be clarified it was out of the Local Conference Committee or Mardy's budget. Keep asking questions so that you are not surprised. The suggestion to have Special Events send out a preconference dinner invitation was made because we felt the quality of the invitations sent out by AOTA was embarrassingly poor, and this Committee would have gladly taken over that responsibility.

Program: Program Committee coordinated well with the Manpower Committee so that volunteers could be contacted efficiently and placed where there was the greatest need for knowledgeable people to man the Speaker's Lounge at all times. Anticipate traffic flow problems and give conveners and door guards a concrete plan to carry out.

Hospitality: Hospitality sets a friendly, welcoming tone to the visitors in your city. Our Committee was extremely creative and resourceful in getting "things" for the Hospitality Room and the amount of space that we were able to give them also contributed to the open, friendly feeling of the displays.

Art Work & Printing: This Committee worked hard to get many tasks accomplished early and yet had to be ready for last minute assignments. The theme and logo of our Conference contributed significantly to its success by its marketability. The quality of all Conference art work was something we were very proud of. The highlight was the back drop, a true engineering feat which displayed our theme and logo all week.

Man Power: What more can we say?! This committee is obviously the backbone of your conference and requires incredible time and energy. It is helpful if the Chairs of this Committee are knowledgeable about your occupational therapy community (facilities, people, etc.) It is critical that Chairs are people who are extremely well organized but flexible enough to accommodate last minute issues.

Public Relations: The quality and diversity of information from this Committee truly helped promote our Conference and Occupational Therapy as a profession. We personally feel the VIP reception was beneficial. It served its purpose with impressive style and grace beyond what had been done previously in our state to acknowledge people who had been supportive of our profession. We had a particular challenge integrating the Local Conference Committee Public Relation Committee with our State Public Relations Committee. They were separate entities by necessity. It might be helpful in future years to identify what the state's true public relation needs might be and gear AOTA Staff help to those needs.

Student: Oregon occupational therapy education includes one OTA Program at Mt. Hood Community College. This provided the Occupational Therapy Assistant students with a marvelous opportunity to demonstrate their skills at planning and presenting at a national professional event. This Committee worked very well and provided the students with a "once in a lifetime" experience. We strongly urge that technical students (OTA) continue to be encouraged as well as asked to participate in this Committee. Communications between the Student Committee and the National Office Liaison and the Director of Conference and Meets was frequently bogged down in misinformation as well as communication blackouts. This made for some rather major last minute changes and multiple frustrations for the Student Committee.

Daily Bulletin: This proved to be a full time job during Conference Week. Insist that Local Conference Committee Chairs get information to the Daily Bulletin Chair ahead of time to be included. The use of just one other person is feasible if you are a high energy and performance Daily Bulletin Chair and have AOTA Staff assistance with typing, stapling, etc.

Job Placement: Remember to orient yourself to the materials before the opening of exhibits. Set up your own system.

Scientific Exhibits: Our Local Conference Committee Scientific Exhibit Chair resigned several weeks before Conference. In dividing those job responsibilities between our Secretary and Treasurer, the tasks were easily accomplished during Conference Week. Details of preliminary work are not available but it seems that an organized person would have little trouble with this Committee. Perhaps the need for Scientific Exhibits needs to be reassessed.

Keep in Mind

1. As a Local Conference Committee Member, it is your job to feed ideas to AOTA and not feel personally offended if they are not accepted.

2. Committee members are not eligible for reimbursement of conference fees. We felt very uncomfortable with this policy

considering the months that many local therapists contributed and suggested that all volunteers are eligible for reimbursement of their conference fees.

3. Humor is a critical ingredient of successful conference. Caution taking yourself too seriously.

4. Enjoy the once in a lifetime opportunity you are embarking on. It is important to enjoy the process of planning the conference as well as the conference itself.

5. Allow everyone an opportunity to do something. There is plenty to do as well as an opportunity for every Occupational Therapy person and facility from your area to shine.

Once again, it has been a delightful experience. It is quite possible that the tardiness of this report is in part due to the inability of the Chair to finalize the closing of the Local Conference Committee with this report. Please do not hesitate to contact us for help or encouragement.

OTAO Staff

The below exerpt is included as a historical account of the major natural disaster that devastated the Pacific NW in the early 1980's, the eruption of Mt. St. Helen's. Coincidentally, this event occurred the same weekend of OTAO in Bend, Oregon. Kay Rhoney, influential OTAO member, recalls her story.

OTAO STATE CONFERENCE   MAY 17-18, 1980

As president of OTAO from 1978 – 80, my last state OT conference was held in Bend, OR. I handed the Presidency to Charlotte DeRenna after a great continuing education event! Two favorite memories of that weekend…First, riding bikes at Sun River with my family (including my parents and 9 month old Suzanne) and Emily Simth and her husband Gordon who rode a "bicycle built for 2" for the first time, but not the last. Second was the explosion of Mt. St. Helens on Sunday 5/18 and all of us seeing the ash plumes as we drove back to Portland.

—Kay Rhoney

© Marianne Kearney. Used with permission.

A full decade of licensure was celebrated in the late 1980's; the state of Oregon acted as the first example of OT licensure in the Pacific Northwest. Many other states followed Oregon's lead in the following years. This piece, written by Sue Nelson, is a thoughtful reflection of how her vision of licensure surpassed her professional expectations.

OCCUPATIONAL THERAPY LICENSING BOARD

10th Year Anniversary

This year, 1988, is a landmark for the Occupational Therapy Licensing Board. It will be ten years this spring since the first licenses were issued to our profession. In the legislative session of 1977, the Occupational Therapy Practice Act was passed and subsequently signed by Governor Bob Straub. A first Board was appointed, and the first executive secretary, Glen Gee, was hired to begin the process of organizing policies and procedures.

Setting up the functions of the licensing systems was an extensive process, and the Board, along with the members of our professional group, each learned about responsibilities to each other. In the beginning years, much effort was spent on communications and public education in order to understand the primary role of licensing as it dealt with consumer protection.

In the early years the Occupational Therapy Licensing Board was one of three boards coordinated by one staff person, which meant our office was operating at about one-third capacity. Gradually as each board grew, our staff position also grew to the current half-time position. Peggy Smith is now the executive secretary of the Occupational Therapy Licensing Board, and she has managed the office and all routine licensing matters since late 1981.

In 1977, Oregon was the seventh state in the country to attain licensure. It has been an extensive four-year process, along with our lobbyist and attorney Kevin O'Connell that led up to the successful outcome.

Every occupational therapist in the state was recruited and played a role in lobbying, writing to legislators (maybe even more than once), having local neighborhood coffee meetings, and in general becoming more informed and more cooperative in a process that required a total team effort. When Senate Bill 791 was signed, everyone felt the accomplishment of a huge goal – a professional milestone as well as the personal satisfaction of energy well spent.

We all learned a lot in the attainment of licensure, and we are all continuing to learn a great deal more through the implementation and interpretation of the statutes. The Licensing Board functions according to responsibilities outlined in those statutes and will continue to develop administrative rules which will further define the statutes.

The Board is empowered by law to monitor the practice of occupational therapy in the state. Recently we have seen how the legislative process and the Licensing Board interact when we participated in the leisure issue with therapeutic recreation personnel. We have also seen how the Licensing Board and the Occupational Therapy Association of Oregon Board and members interact when participating in a process of mutual concern to occupational therapists and therapeutic recreationists. When we all work together towards a common goal it takes a lot of coordination and cooperation, and we can again see how that efficient team process can lead toward the attainment of another goal and resolution of professional concerns.

As we celebrate our tenth anniversary, I'd like to thank you all again for the continued involvement with legislative issues and for the effective interaction between our groups. It has been a real learning experience and a process that will continue to develop and become more sophisticated as we work towards a further common understanding of our political system. The statutes that define occupational therapy practice in Oregon are the foundation for our profession and apply to all of us.

The celebration of the tenth anniversary of the licensing process does not affect just the Licensing Board, but affects the accomplishments of the Occupational Therapy Association of Oregon as well and the ways that you have impacted professional licensing.

Susan C. Nelson, OTR/L, Chairperson
Occupational Therapy Licensing Board of Oregon

8

Pacific University: 1990-1999

Pacific University Boxer: The Boxer represents cultural diversity and embodiment of community. This mysterious dragon-like creature has been a symbol of Pacific University since 1896. This is the most current version of the logo, designed in 2008. Used with permission.

> **To** Lilian
> **Date** 1-20-82   **Time** 10:00
>
> ## WHILE YOU WERE OUT
>
> **Mr.** Tom Griffith
> **of** Pacific University
> **Phone** 357-6151 x 233
>
> | Telephoned | | Please Call | ✓ |
> |---|---|---|---|
> | Called to See You | | Will Call Again | ✓ |
> | Wants to See You | | Ret'd Your Call | |
>
> **Message:** Faculty Approved the O.T. Proposal
>
> **MT. HOOD COMMUNITY COLLEGE**

This memo is one that I received at Mt. Hood Community College when I was employed as the Director/Coordinator of the Occupational Therapy Assistant Program. The message was from Tom Griffith, Physics Professor at Pacific University. He was one of the primary people (also Carol Schunk, PT and Dean Malcolm) that Kay Rhoney and myself were working with to explore the possibility of developing a school of occupational therapy at Pacific University. —Lilian Crawford. Used with permission.

Pacific University continues to educate students and practitioners by exposing people to a variety of settings and populations in which occupational therapy flourishes. The below article is a good example of how occupational therapist have embedded skills in a variety of professions.

Below is a comparison of OTAO membership between 1996 and 2016. Efforts to increase awareness and membership are still of peak interest for OTAO.

OTAO Membership Roster 1996

Registered Occupational Therapists: 300

Certified Occupational Therapy Assistants: 56

Honorary Members: 10

Occupational Therapy Students: 33

Occupational Therapy Asst. Students: 10

Associate Members: 2

Total: 411

OTAO Membership Roster 2016

Registered Occupational Therapists: 177

Certified Occupational Therapy Assistants: 25

Honorary Members: 6

Students (OTR & COTA): 94

Total: 208

Traditionally, graduated cohorts from Pacific University present a gift to the faculty. The below description is a reminder of where one can find more information about OTAO's rich history.

Class of 1998 Explores "The Roots of OTAO"

—Cameron Smith, OTS

To celebrate the 50-year anniversary of the Occupational Therapy Association of Oregon, students from the class of 1998 created a collection of videos called "The Roots of OTAO". The project, which consisted of interviews with occupational therapists who shaped the OTAO from 1947-1977, was presented at the 1997 Annual Conference last October. Walter Ludtke, a pioneer of the Mt. Hood Community College COTA program, and Jean Vann, the third president of OTAO, came up with the project idea when they met at the OTAO Conference in 1996. Recognizing the importance of understanding the roots of OT in Oregon, we were honored to be asked to complete such a project.

Each student asked four main questions in the interviews. They were: 1) What was the OTAO like when you joined? 2) What did you do as a member of the association? 3) What issues were present at the time? 4) What changes have you noticed in the OTAO and the OT field? OT students who participated included Jay Wheeler, Connie Whittier, Angie Anderson, Julie Allen, Erica Amundson, Nicole Hew and Cameron Smith. The therapists interviewed were: Ruth Ann Moore, Jean Vann, Walter Ludtke, Lois Walsh, Linda Johnson, Dixie Arata, Sue Nelson, Bonnie Harwood, Connie Weiss, Norma Holliman, Linda Armstrong, Patricia Evans, Karen Foley, Wenda Lloyd, Kay Rhoney, Pauline Petterson, and Evelyn Brill.

Each of us had very different experiences as we set out with video cameras, microphones and maps of the countryside to meet with our assigned occupational therapists. Jay Wheeler and I even had the pleasure of joining Jean Vann on a road trip to Corvallis and Newport where we interviewed her old cronies; Walter Ludtke, Lois

Wlsh, and Linda Johnson. As those of you who have worked with Jean in the past might have guessed, she came prepared for the trip. Jean brought a cooler full of food for everyone and the stories she told during our time together were amazing!

Looking back on the interview process, I realize the incredible value of the experience. We learned about how each therapist contributed to the creation and growth of the OTAO community and we learned about how each therapist spends his/her time today.

"The Roots of OTAO" video series is now a part of the video archives at the OTAO office. Please feel free to check them out if you are interested in learning more about the individuals who built the foundation of our state association!

Pacific University's School of Occupational Therapy

Impact of Education on Practice

Molly McEwen. Used with permission.

In the mid-20th century, Oregon occupational therapy practitioners began to realize the value of having a professional educational program within the state. Jean Vann, OTR, Virginia Hatch, OTR, and Shirley Bowing, OTR were just a few of the therapists who invested time and energy over the years on promoting this endeavor. In 1948, in an effort to determine program feasibility, members of the state association began contacting other professional programs in the region as well as major facilities and institutions in determining the current and future need for occupational therapists. Between 1947 and 1970, the University of Oregon in Eugene, the University of Oregon Medical School (now OHSU), and Portland State University were presented with the resultant needs study for consideration. No interest was generated.

In 1976, Pacific University contacted the AOTA to explore the possibility of establishing a professional entry-level baccalaureate program. Sue Nelson, OTR, as the President of OTAO, began meeting with Dean Malcolm (Dean of the College of Arts and Sciences, Pacific University) and appointed an advisory committee to assist the University in exploring the possibility of developing a program. After some consideration, the issue was given inactive status due to questionable visability.

In 1979, Lilan Crawford, MOT, OTR and Kay Rhoney, OTR (then President of OTAO) again approached Pacific University and reactivated the process. At that time, Pacific University had two health professional programs: Optometry and Physical Therapy. Dr. Tom Griffith, Chair of the Science Division, chaired a committee consisting of representatives from the College of Arts and Sciences faculty and administration. With new information on the development and role of the profession and an updated needs assessment, new enthusiasm was generated that led to the development of a proposal to begin a professional entry-level baccalaureate (OTR) program along side the physical therapy program within the College of Arts and Sciences. Presented to the University Faculty Senate in January 1982, the proposal was approved, and then forwarded to the Curriculum Committee and ultimately the Board of Trustees for final approval and establishment of a task force to solicit start-up funds through grants and supporting organizations.

Delvina Gross, PhD, OTR was recruited as the Director, starting September 1983 and Tina Fletcher, MFA, OTR was hired as the first full-time faculty member. The first class of 18 students was admitted to the program, housed in the basement of Walter Hall (dormitory) beginning in the fall of 1984. In 1985, Lilian Crawford, MOT, OTR was hired to complete the first team of full-time faculty. The initial accreditation process by the AOTA was successfully completed in spring of 1986 and the first class of students graduated in May of that year.

Due to health considerations, Delvina Gross, PhD, OTR resigned from her position beginning September 1986, and left the program in January 1987. Molly McEwen, MHS, OTR, joined the faculty in fall 1986 and assumed the Acting Director role in spring 1987. During her tenure as Director (1987-2001), significant trends and healthcare legislation influenced the practice of occupational therapists and subsequently professional entry-level education.

The 1980's brought legislative changes in healthcare with specific emphasis on cost containment. The system of prospective payment was implemented and resulted in a transition from hospital-based acute medical care to greater personal responsibility, self-care and home health programs. Hospital stays and treatment were greatly shortened with patients returning to the community much sooner. This was an opportunity for OT to practice in the more natural/non-medical environments of individuals served. This approach resonated with the founding philosophy and values of the profession. New service delivery models developed. Preparation of entry-level occupational therapists necessitated the examination of requirements for professional practice in a new health care environment.

Pacific's program, well positioned in a liberal arts and science university, embraced a more holistic community-based approach to practice while still maintaining hospital-based opportunities. Collaboration with the arts and sciences community fostered a broader basis for understanding the power of the art and science of occupation leading to health [ie, interdisciplinary work within the school of health professions and community service projects]. Curricular revision occurred with the school successfully completing its second accreditation process in 1991, being cited positively for a "cutting edge" curriculum.

In the 1990's, the profession continued to find its place with other major health care professions. Greater emphasis emerged on the need for systematic research necessary to support practice and clearly establish special expertise. Practice continued to expand into varied environments of the client's life [ie, expanding into community settings, developing programing to support underserved populations, return-to-work initiatives, and home health programs]. Landmark legislation substantially changed opportunities for social participation of people with disabilities. This provided even great opportunity of occupational therapy practice within the community. The ability of the practitioner to successfully practice in emerging areas as well as the increasingly demanding traditional health care environments required more sophisticated skill sets.

Entry-level baccalaureate curricula continued to add more and more content to meet the changing demands of practice. At this time, the profession began encouraging expansion to graduate entry-level and a mandate for graduate entry-level was visible on the distant horizon. The School of Occupational Therapy took a pro-active stance and began developing an entry-level Master's program with greater emphasis on preparing students for evidenced-based practice and with the ability to adapt to the quickly changing environment of health-care delivery. An integrated curriculum requiring faculty collaboration and teaming for teaching and mentoring was implemented. Core content was sequenced and threaded through multiple courses, thereby curricular content was organized in a more integrated manner. Fieldwork was re-designed, working closely with community practitioners.

The first MOT class was admitted in 1997. Students were prepared with strong clinical reasoning and clinical research skills for traditional and non-traditional areas of practice, and with the ability to develop and market programs within emerging practice areas within the community. The new curricular organization was successfully accredited in spring 2000, with the first class graduating that year.

1998 brought the Balanced Budget Act that began to influence professional job opportunities and subsequently student enrollments, nationwide. With the cost of education increasing and job potential compromised, applicant pools dropped significantly throughout the nation during the course of approximately 5 years. Pacific was no exception to this trend.

After 13 years, Molly McEwen stepped down from the director

position in 2000, yet agreed to maintain the role until an appropriate replacement was found to guide the program into the new millennium. In fall 2002, John White, PhD, OTR was hired to assume the director role.

White's tenure brought a professional discussion regarding yet another level of entry into the profession, a clinical doctorate. In an effort to be prepared for future demand for services, some believe that entry-level clinical doctorate requirements enable the profession to evolve developmentally and to remain viable in the deliverance of health and human services. A doctorate also aligns the profession with other allied health professionals. While a clinical doctorate is not currently mandated, debate continues regarding a possible clinical doctorate mandate or for the need for multiple options for entry into the profession. In response to current tends and demands on the practitioner, Pacific University, School of Occupational Therapy initiated a clinical doctorate program in 2012. The MOT program was phased out with the last class graduating in 2014.

Peggy Hanson, Interim Director, 2000-2003

In 2000, following Molly McEwan's announcement that she would step down from the position, the School of OT began actively searching for a new program director. A search committee had been formed and candidates interviewed by none seemed to be the right fit. This was a time of uncertainty within the profession, not just in Oregon, but nation wide, and significant changes in reimbursement systems were impacting the entire profession. OT programs were experiencing a serious decline in student applications and faculty were hesitant to leave secure positions. These trends had not gone unnoticed by Pacific University's administration and some members of the search committee were concerned about the University's commitment to the process.

In response, the provost decided that a review of the program was needed to assess the school's current needs and future viability. Two university administrators and an occupational therapist were asked to serve on the review committee. At its first meeting, two of the committee members agreed that with decreasing enrollment and an unsuccessful search the outlook was not hopeful. However, the occupational therapist on the committee, Peggy Hanson OTR/L argued that the current situation needed to be understood within the larger context of challenges facing the profession and its potential to successfully adapt. After collecting data from all stakeholders, vising other OT programs and consulting with AOTA advisors, the review committee ultimately was convinced and made a strong case for the programs continuation and future potential. The committee's final report, presented in the fall of 2001, included the recommendation that an interim Program Director be appointed with specific short term goals for the program, while temporarily suspending the search for a permanent director.

In January 2002 Hanson was asked to serve in the interim director position. For the next 18 months, she and the faculty worked to meet the goals to increase enrollment and stabilize the faculty. At almost the same time, the school received notice that NBCOT had lowered the programs accreditation to a probationary status until they could meet the standards for facility and classroom resources. This required working closely with National Board for Certification in Occupational Therapy (NBCOT) to provide the necessary documentation and also put an additional strain on achieving the goals set by the university. However, by the beginning of the 2002-2003 academic year, the program was making good progress and the search for a permanent director was reopened.

The 2003 academic year ended with full accreditation status reinstated, enrollment goals met, a stable faculty in place and John White, PHD, OTR/L accepting the position of permanent program director. During this challenging time, the OT practice community, and OTAO supported the School of Occupational Therapy in many ways. Especially significant to this success was a cadre of practioners who served as temporary advisory group to the interim director establishing the foundation for the strong advisory board that exists today.

—Molly McEwen

Pacific University School of OT History 1995-2015

John White. Used with permission.

The School of Occupational Therapy at Pacific University was established as a Bachelor of Science in OT degree program in 1984, graduating the charter class of students in 1986. Delvina Gross, PhD was the founding program director and supported the initial accreditation of the program and was succeeded by Molly McEwen, MSOT, FAOTA, who served as program director until 2001. Alumna Peggy Hansen (Class of 1991) served as interim program director until 2003, when John White, PhD, FAOTA, assumed the director's role. A new director took over Pacific OT leadership in July of 2015, Dr. Gregory Wintz, Ph. D., OTR/L.

The school's leadership has been consistently recognized for innovation in curricular development and design. The school has an excellent record of accreditation of the program with each new degree offerings through the years (1984-98: BSOT, 2000-14: MOT, & 2015 forward: OTD).

Debate about the most appropriate degree for entry-level OT education began around 1950 when Mary Reilly, supported by prominent OT leaders such as Wilma West and Florence Cromwell, encouraged the profession move to the entry-level master's degree. By the 1990s the debate continued and choosing to lead the trend,

Director Molly McEwen and faculty elected to transition the BSOT to a Master of Occupational Therapy degree and admitted the first Master Degree of Occupational Therapy (MOT) students in 1997 and the program was lengthened to a 3 year graduating cycle to replace the 2 year Bachelor of Science cycle. Therefore there was no graduating class for 1999, and the charter class of MOT graduates received their diplomas in May of 2000.

The move to the MOT was visionary in that by 1999, the AOTA Representative Assembly passed Resolution J: "Movement to Required Postbaccalaureate Level of Education" which eventually led to the requirement for all entry-level programs had to move to a post-baccalaureate level by January 2007.

In preparation for the next accreditation by ACOTE, the MOT curriculum was revised under the direction of John White and implemented in 2007, the same year the program received a 10-year reaccreditation status.

By 2006, several Universities were offering an entry-level Doctor of Occupational Therapy (OTD) degree and that year the Accreditation Council of Occupational Therapy Education (ACOTE) published the first educational standards for OT doctorate programs. By 2010, the School of OT faculty was in regular discussion about the pros and cons of adopting the Doctor of OT degree (OTD) as the new entry-level requirement. Continuing the visionary trend set at Pacific, the Director and faculty opted to significantly revise the curriculum and in 2011 proposed to the University that the School of OT move to the entry-level OTD, and simultaneously offer a post-professional OTD *(POTD). The innovative hybrid curriculum integrated distance based (online) coursework into the program that provided students more flexible living arrangements in their third year. The charter OTD Class of 2015 was admitted in the fall of 2012 and OT commencement changed from May to August. Pacific University was the 7th in the U.S. to be accredited to offer the entry-level OTD when it received full accreditation from ACOTE in December of 2014 (for the maximum available time period of 7 years).

Due to low enrollment numbers, the POTD program was suspended and stopped admitting new post-professional students after the fall of 2014.

Further affirmation of the transition to the OTD came in the spring of 2014 when the AOTA Board of Directors issued a position paper recommending that the profession move to doctoral entry-level by 2025. The position paper cited the probable benefits to the profession of an educational process that would lead to a more independent practitioner whose entry-level skills had been enhanced by a culminating 16 week experiential internship in a focused practice area. The capstone project that accompanies the internship provides the student with in-depth and advanced knowledge in the chosen area.

Highly qualified and deeply committed faculty over the years have assured that innovations and advances in education as championed by Pacific's School of OT have prepared forward-thinking practitioners to help shape a rapidly-changing healthcare landscape. The school has also been graced with dedicated, caring, and talented administrative staff who have assured smooth operations over the years.

—John White

OREGON OCCUPATIONAL THERAPY LICENSING BOARD

20th Year Anniversary

1997

What an exhilarating coincidence that we can celebrate the 50th year anniversary of OTAO as well as the 20th year anniversary of Oregon licensure.

Ten years ago when I wrote a Viewpoint article about the licensing ten year anniversary, I was somewhat in awe of our accomplishments and the extensive process of the licensing system. Now, in 1997, I am still in awe of our professional and regulatory growth, and still never cease to be challenged and excited about the licensure areas.

Have we change in the last 20 years? We certainly have!! The first 123 licensing applications were submitted to the original Licensing Board. This year the Board has issued 1200 licenses to occupational therapists and occupational therapy assistants. When the Board was first set up, there were to be 16 Board meetings a year. Once the regulations were written, the application packet was put together, and all the lists were made to notify the occupational therapy community, the Licensing Board meetings were reduced to 10 a year. Now, and for a long time, the Board meetings are held quarterly, and usually one meeting a year is held around the state, at least out of the Portland area.

What kinds of issues has the Board dealt with?

1. Qualifications for licensure applicants

2. Development of the limited permit

3. Recreation therapy issues – begun in 1982, with a redefining of our word "leisure" in our administrative rule. The situation ended with a confrontational experience in a legislative hearing the eventually was reached by mutual agreement with the therapeutic recreation people.

4. Continuing education requirements were on the agenda nearly every Board meeting since 1979. Mandatory CE requirements for renewal applications became effective in 1994 and now include guidelines for mentorship for persons whose license has lapsed for more than three years.

5. Geri Aman, current OTAO President, was active in 1984 and became involved through her practice in helping the Board develop administrative rules regarding occupational therapy practice for children in school systems.

6. Since 1990 the Board dealt with many legislative efforts to eliminate regulatory boards, especially the health related licensing boards. In 1990 through 1993, it was the Sunset Review Process. In 1994, it was governor Roberts' Reorganization Process, and "downsizing state government." Last year, it was the PEW Report that became an extensive threat to licensing as we know it, and the national trend towards privatization of many licensing services.

But through all the history of our past 20 years, the primary focus of the OT Licensing Baord has continued to be the protection of the public – our clients – the consumer of our professional services.

How do we fare in carrying out the primary directive?

The Board has processed complaints of patient injury, inappropriate treatment procedures and of inappropriate physical contact with clients. Also, there have been instances of persons working without a license, false documentation of credentials, unprofessional communication with patients, and questions of ethical supervisory procedures.

The occupational therapy licensing/regulatory statures are the laws of the state of Oregon. It is an on-going process to be a watchdog of our patients and also to monitor ethical and professional services delivery through the legislative and regulatory process.

I hope I am still around, as well as the licensure process, to see what it will all look like for the 30th year anniversary. I expect there will be many changes and surprises.

In the meantime, congratulations to all of you here today who were involved in the original legislative efforts and who also continue to work in collaboration with OTAO and the Licensing Board, and who continue to strive for professional excellence.

History of OT Advisory Board

The school of OT at Pacific University continues to support efforts of the advisory board; below is a brief history to frame the incredible work and dedication of the group.

The Pacific University School of OT Advisory board was re-formed in 2005 under new director John A. White, Jr., Ph.D., OTR/L. An earlier version existed when the School of OT was started in the mid 1980's but was loosely formed and ceased to exist by the early 1990's. This new Advisory Board was established as an additional source of advice and support as the school headed into its first accreditation since John had become Director. The first pool of members was selected by John from known supports of the school. Sherry Hoff, long term adjunct then associate professor now community advocate was asked and agreed to be the first chair. She and John agreed on and asked Sue Nelson to be the vice-chair and Secretary. The group was established as non-fiduciary thus there is no Treasurer.

Of note is that no other Allied Health School at Pacific University had an advisory board at that time thus the model established, along with the guidelines and mission, had to be created from scratch and were thus the primary topic of discussion and work through most of the first year. Subsequently topics have focused on growth and development of the school as it transitioned into the OTD curriculum, establishing ongoing connections and collaborations between the school of OT and other organizations, such as OTAO, and perpetuation of the Audrey Kerseg Fund for permanence and growth of scholarship for students. Out of all of this has come a few traditions, one of which is the eagerly awaited winter meeting when students present their first hand photos and reports from their exciting fieldwork journeys to Nicaragua, China, Bangladesh, and South Africa.

The group consists of community OT practitioners, community

therapy leaders of any discipline, and students selected by merit from class volunteers. Originally formatted with committees, the group soon became more centralized with all members having a voice on all topics with little intermittent between-meeting work. The current model of this Advisory Board is quite nontraditional. This is, by design, a very open style board. By agreement of 100% of the members, topics can be brought before the board from any member, and the school director, with no topic, no matter how potentially sensitive to the program or an individual, discussed in secret.

Membership is asked to be for a 4-year term. The size has remained relatively stable at 14-16. Dynamics of course evolve with changes in membership. Please see the list of current and past dedicated volunteers. As the Advisory Board moved forward, Sue Nelson stepped up in 2008 when Sherry developed a temporary medical condition. Sherry resumed chair in 2012 and Sue Nelson retired with honors and thanks. Dona Schumacher has been vice-Chair and great thread through that transition and will retire in 2014. The Board continues with exuberance and dynamism.

MISSION STATEMENT: To advise and support the School of Occupational Therapy in its endeavor of recruitment, development, and promotion of students and the profession.

*Courtesy of the School of OT newsletter

The below example is a good representation of how the advisory board has affected both personal and professional lives. Pacific University continues to honor members of the advisory board through program and scholarship development.

Advisory Board 2014

Sherry Hoff visits with Kevin Gardner ('97) and Angelique Gardner ('97) in Ireland. Courtesy of: Pacific University School of Occupational Therapy. Used with permission.

Life is all about transitions, and occupational therapy is about helping others through those changes. I, Sherry Hoff, have taken my own advice to many of my patients and have started establishing myself in a position to age optimally. For me that means a move to be near family in Boise, Idaho. Thus I have resigned as Chair of the School of Occupational Therapy Advisory Board.

The new, and incredibly worthy, Chair is Kelli Iranshad, OTR/L. A graduate of the Class of 1997, Kelli is a familiar face among all of the subsequent classes through her continued participation in school coursework and activities.

As the Advisory Board matures the evident need for our action grows. The communication and interaction between school and community is a vital piece, as is the community of local OT's potential for contribution to the school. The Board is a direct link to each and poised for action.

As I leave the essential world of OT it will never leave me. I can see my role to advocate for the exciting growth of our profession through mentorship and modeling. I would encourage all of you reading this to take your profession seriously. To make it more of who you are and support all arenas through attendance and voluntary action. Each of you is an important voice.

We wish you the best, Sherry! Thank you for your service and tireless efforts to promote occupational therapy. Further changes on the board include Dona Schumacher, class of '87, former vice chair; and Jeff Roehm who rotated off in April 2014, Rebecca Pence is the new vice chair.

—Sherry Hoff

9
The New Millennium

© Painting by Daniel Tautenhan, LMT, MBA, OTD, Pacific University Class of 2017. Used with permission.

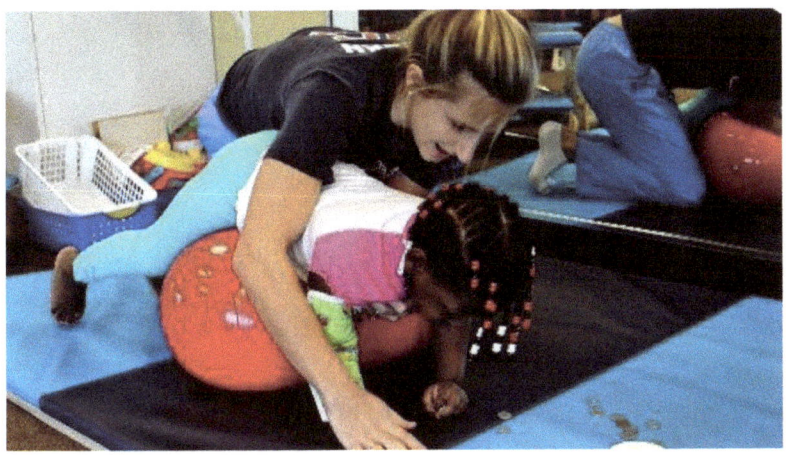

Image from Linn-Benton Community College. Used with permission.

Linn-Benton Community College (LBCC)

The LBCC Occupational Therapy Assistant program is a two-year Associate of Applied Science Degree program accredited by the Accreditation Council for Occupational Therapy Education. The program follows a hybrid delivery model and includes classroom, laboratory, and fieldwork components.
Used with permission

- Classroom: Traditional students attend classes in person on the LBCC campus while distance-education students attend classes in real time/at the same time via the internet.

- Laboratory: Traditional students attend labs on the LBCC campus while distance-education students attend labs at partner community colleges or other sites in their geographic area. Additionally, all students come to the LBCC campus for one-day or two-day visits up to three times per term. Students are responsible for all associated travel costs.

- Fieldwork: Fieldwork experiences are completed at fieldwork sites in the Pacific Northwest; fieldwork placement is determined by the Academic Fieldwork Coordinator and is dependent upon availability of fieldwork sites and educators. Students are responsible for all associated travel costs.

A cohort of 24 students is admitted to each class. Students will develop an understanding of occupational therapy theory and practice, including activity analysis and clinical reasoning for helping clients meet their goals. Successful graduates will be eligible and prepared to sit for the national certification examination and to function as entry-level occupational therapy assistants in a variety of practice settings.

Written by: Ann Custer

Courtesy of: www.linnbenton.edu/ota

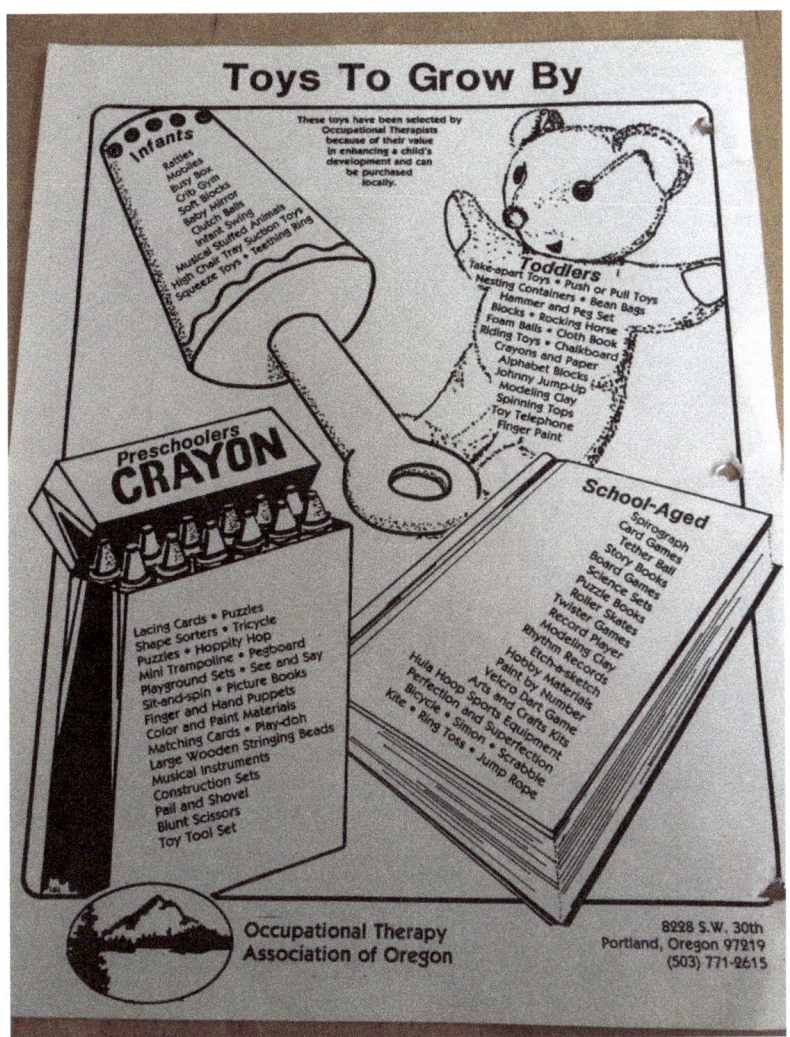

© OTAO Viewpoint. Used with permission.

Animal-Assisted Therapy Note – 1995

Andrea Wall, OTR and her certified Delta Therapy dog Rusty appeared on MCTV several times in January. The topic was OT and animal assisted activities and therapy. A copy of the program will be made available to the OT library.

Andrea Wall has been an OTR for over 23 years. She feels fortunate to be able to find a way to combine her profession with her love of dogs. As a volunteer for the PPPP (Prison Pet Partnership Program), she was asked by Jeanne Hample to perform an OT evaluation of Maggie, who had applied to receive an assistance dog. She was able to determine that Maggie had the upper body strength to arise from the floor or a chair when pushing up from a dog height object, and also that retrieving objects from the floor and carrying a pack would help her become more independent. She also felt Maggie could benefit from an assistance dog to help her balance on stairs and level surfaces. Maggie appeared to have the motivation, ability and family support to benefit from an assistance dog.

According to the Delta Society Service Dog Center in Renton, Washington, ". . . of the 50 million people with disabilities in the United States, only about 14,000 are currently benefiting from service dogs." Most service dog training programs have a five-year waiting list. More disabled people are having dogs trained privately or by small programs such as the PPPP.

10
Quilts

Teresa Fairfield Quilt. Pacific University School of Occupational Therapy.

It occurred to me to make this quilt as a dedication to my profession nearly as soon as I began quilting. A quilt seemed the perfect medium to express the profession of occupational therapy. Each element of the quilt reflects an aspect of this work and a blend of old and new from the composition, fabrics, quilting methods, block design and batting, and especially the process.

If any words were to describe the profession of occupational therapy, growth, labor, exploration, and art do. The red house is Growth. It depicts the seeds of planting around fields and homes in America. Look for watermelon, sunflower, tomato and carrot. The green house is Labor and reflects the tools used to plant these seeds: shovels, hoes, and rakes. The blue house is Exploration, for the traveler. Gloves, binoculars, maps and old-fashioned cameras are all tools used for exploration. The black house is Art, made for the artist, for the creative expression of each of us. It contains a palette, paint tubes, easels, brushes, pencils, compasses and architectural triangles. You'll notice that the doors and windows, the part of a house that joins its inhabitants to the outside world, now stand out from the houses themselves, allowing the viewer access to the quilt; the gold brings us closer in. The outer border, binding, and backing is red with black fleck detail, the colors of Pacific University, home for this quilt.

The following essay was written and submitted by a Pacific University student to accompany a beautiful quilt. This is a great example of how students use their own creative occupations to explain what the profession means to them and the greater community.

Being an alumna of the Pacific University School of Occupational Therapy Class of 1993, this, the year 1996, finds me three years out from that graduation date. Many things come easier to me now than they did as a new grad, working as the only occupational therapist in a community re-entry neuro-behavioral setting. Many lessons are still coming. Similarly, this quilt is far from perfection.

There are many things I could have taken out, redone. I chose not to. However, the mistakes represent my quilting skills at this time, already improved over my early skills.

In my lifetime I will make many quilts; with each quilting, I learn something new and become better at the task. Likewise, in my profession, the lessons are still coming. The therapist that I am and the treatment I provide is also a work in progress. Like this quilt, with each new client I see, I piece together a picture that becomes more whole and complete with each piece, but at the same time, has never been incomplete. It is like piecing a quilt top, there's nothing missing, it just becomes more with each addition. I already look back to my days as a brand new therapist. My construction looks crude to me, yet a representation of my skills at the time. I cannot even see ahead to a time when I will look back to the place where I am now. But I know it will come.

Look on this quilt. Find yourself here somewhere. Get up close and pick out one piece, a tiny one, maybe the trunk of a tree or part of a house. When you feel like the skills you have now aren't enough, think about this: This piece is where you are right now. If you're constructing a life the way I constructed this quilt, the whole quilt depends on this tiny piece. Look at the neighboring pieces, look at the pieces next to those, and next to those. See the tiny stitches. Zillions of them. Recognize the fact that the entire quilt, everything that holds it together, is stitched to that tiny piece; the where you are now, tiny piece. If you can stand it, stand back and look at the whole thing, your life. Each moment, each new experience, adds another piece. Some are big, some small, some brightly colored, some shades of beige, and some dark. The pieces make a block, the blocks make a segment, the segments are sashed together, the sashing is connected to an inner border, an outer border, batting and a back. Here is your quilt, your life, your profession.

I quilt because I like stitching together tiny pieces to make something glorious. I am an occupational therapist because I like stitching together tiny pieces to make something glorious. Now you see why I donate this quilt to Pacific University. I used to have a pile of cut patches. Now I have a quilt. Where do you think I got my "sewing machine?"

—Teresa Fairfield

O.T. Historical Quilt Project

This quilt depicts 30 years of occupational therapy development in Oregon. Practitioners represented by each of the squares were actively involved in leadership roles with OTAO between 1947 and 1977. Students from Pacific University teamed with some of the therapists in creating the individual squares. The quilt was presented to Pacific University School of Occupational Therapy upon its completion in May 2000.

Pacific University School of Occupational Therapy

Class of 2000 – Historical Quilt Project

The following are the names of the practitioners and students participating in the commemorative quilt.

Please note that the biographies described in this chapter were written near the quilt's completion in the year 2000. Updated information from today's perspective may not have been included.

Practitioners	Students
Geri Arman	Caroline Quist
Ruth Ann Moore	Christine Corey
Dixie Arata	Joanna Blanchard
Elizabeth Callahan	Stacey Moret
Lilian Crawford	Dana Matteucci
Karen Foley	Amy Anderson
Marilyn Forse	Chris Erickson
Kai Galyen	Corina Fisher
Bonnie Harwood	Susan Zaragoza
Norma Holliman	Jeff Gaschler
Linda Johnson	Karen Nagao
Sue Knapp (Milton)	Julie Droomgoole
Walt Ludke	Sarah Saxton-Buckholz
Molly McEwen	Naomi Ishikawa
Sue Nelson	
Pauline Petterson	
Kay Rhoney	
Jean Vann	
Cathy Vorheis	
Connie Weise	
Lois Walsh	
Pat Evans	

	OT Creating Quilt Square	OTS from Pacific University
Row 1	Marilyn Forse	Chris Erickson
	Sue Nelson	Julie Droomgoole
	Sue Milton Knapp	Corina Fisher
	Walt Ludtke	Caroline Quist
Row 2	Lois Walsh	
	Karen Foley	Amy Anderson
	Cathy Vorhies	
	Pauline Petterson	Susan Saragoza
Row 3	Bonnie Harwood	Susan Saragoza
	Picture of new O.T. School	Susan Saragoza
	Geri Arman	Caroline Quist
	Kay Rhoney	
Row 4	Connie Weiss	Naomi Ishikawa
	Molly McEwen	Susan Saragoza
	Seal of Pacific University	Susan Saragoza
	Elizabeth Callahan	Stacey Moret
Row 5	Ruth Ann Moore	Christine Corey
	Jean Vann	Sarah Saxton
	Kai Gaylen	Corina Fisher
	Dixie Arata	Joanna Blanchard
Row 6	Norma Holliman	Jeff Gaschler
	Lilian Crawford	Dana Matteucci
	Pat Evans	
	Linda Johnson	Karen Nagao

O.T.s in the Historical OTAO Quilt Project
Individual Squares

Row 1 (Left to Right)

Marilyn Forse:

Marilyn graduated from Washington University, St. Louis, MO in 1946. In OTAO she served as treasurer in 1965 and 1966, as secretary in 1970 and 1971, and with a variety of committees, including fund raising. OT work included rehabilitation, physical disabilities, pediatrics, geriatric, and a nursing home consultant. Quilt Square's Philosophy is "Do everything you can to help the patient and do no harm." Also, included is therapeutic use of self.

Sue Nelson:

Sue graduated from the University of Minnesota in 1953. In OTAO Sue served as president in 1976-1977, during which there was a push to establish an O.T. Licensing Board. The bill to established O.T. Licensing Board was passed in 1977. Sue served on the Licensing Board in 1997. OT work was mostly pediatrics, working with the blind children, cerebral palsy, Down's Syndrome, and consultants to school district. She is currently working as an advisor to SOTA at Pacific University's O.T. school. The quilt Square represents herself and work experience. Mt. Hood is a symbol of striving for excellence, and the seal represents her job as SOTA advisor.

Sue Milton Knapp:

Sue graduated from the University of Puget Sound in Tacoma in 1970. In OTAO she served as Membership Chair 1971-1972, as Directory Chair on 1972-1973, Treasurer 1973-1976, and other various committees. OT work includes, pediatrics, psychiatry, physical disabilities, home health, and traveling OT, which she is currently doing. The quilt Square represents collaboration with patients and client centered outcomes, as well as friends she has made. The wheelchair represents her brother who was disabled in an accident and was an inspiration to her.

Walt Ludtke:

Walt graduated from the University of Puget Sound in 1956. In OTAO he served as president in 1968-1969. He also served on various committees. OT work was in psychiatry at a VA hospital and teaching classes. In 1967, he came to Portland and headed the new OTA program at Mt. Hood Community College. The quilt Square represents establishing the OTA program at Mt. Hood Community College.

Row 2 (Left to Right)

Lois Walsh:

Lois graduated from Western Michigan College in 1945. In OTAO she did publicity and served on various committees. OT work was in pediatrics. In Los Angeles, she developed two programs at Orthopedic Hospital. At the Holladay Center for Handicapped Children Lois worked doing OT in the school, taught Home Economics, Industrial Arts, and worked with teachers. She was the second OT at this school. She did research on measuring ocular pursuits with Colorado State and presenting this at the AOTA Conference in Los Angeles. At PSU, she helped teach special education teachers. The quilt square reflects Lois's work at the Holladay Center.

Karen Foley:

Karen graduated from Indiana University in 1945. In OTAO she served as state representatives to AOTA for 18 years, beginning in 1980. This is a record for holding this office. OT work is in physical disabilities and administration. In 1978, Karen established the OT Department at St. Vincent's Hospital. The department grew and Karen is the Director of Rehabilitation Services. Her quilt square includes a green spider web which represents all things connected. Symbols that are on it are: a fish tank that represents community, the heart represents passion, the hands represent helping others, the telescope represents visions of the future, the bag represents skills, and the word "know" represents Karen's Welch heritage.

Cathy Vorhies:

Cathy graduated from the University of Toronto in 1976. In OTAO she was the chair of legislative committee, and spearheaded an effort to get OT as mandatory insurance coverage in Oregon. She was also the chair of continuing education. In 1979-1980 she held office of vice president, and later was elected president of OTAO in the 1980's. Cathy held office of representative for the AOTA. Cathy also worked as chair of a state annual conference planning committee. For 4.5 years she served on the Licensing Board. OT work was varied. She worked at a psychiatric day center, in acute physical disabilities, in both in and out patient care, long term care/geriatrics, and teaching classes at both Mt. Hood Community College and Pacific University. The quilt square includes three books that represent her contribution to OTAO. The OTAO policies and procedures were organized and written by Cathy. She found and hired the executive secretary for the OTAO, establishing a business office. The bookends were given to Cathy at Pacific University for being a distinguished volunteer. The red geranium represents her love for gardening. The window represents looking out in the world of opportunities as well as her enjoyment of the outdoors.

Pauline Petterson:

Pauline graduated from Mount Mary College, Milwaukee, Wisconsin in 1967. In OTAO she has been chair of fundraising, program chairman, council of practice chair, and vice president 1974-1975. Pauline is currently vice president and SIS coordinator. OT work began with 2 years as OT in the U.S. Navy, serving as lieutenant. She has worked in physical disabilities for 20 years. She has worked in out patient, rehab, industrial medicine, workmen's comp., and ergonomics. Quilt Square consists of navy blue and gold stripes representing the Navy. The Kaiser emblem, where she worked for 20 years, represents both her personal family and the Kaiser Family. The letters OTAO represent her involvement in the association. Her Campfire name is ONKA-CHUTA which means to help in sickness with hand. The mountain signifies Oregon as well as the OT in Oregon.

Row 3 (Left to Right)

Bonnie Harwood:

Bonnie graduated from the University of Puget Sound in 1955. In OTAO Bonnie served as president in 1972-1973. It was during the first year of Bonnie's term of office that a bylaws change came, making all one year offices to two years. She was on the committee to instigate this change. OT work has been mostly home health and nursing home environment. The quilt square's philosophy represents teamwork in an environment of change.

Pacific University School of Occupational Therapy Square

Geri Aman:

Geri was leading OTAO into the year 2000 as the president of OTAO. Geri graduated from the University of Puget sound in 1977. In OTAO she has been on the Executive Board since 1980. Geri served as president from 1996-2000. OT work has been primarily in the pediatric area, including being a school therapist. The quilt square's philosophy is how OT has provided many opportunities that would not have been available with OT and able to expand herself as a person as well as in the field of OT.

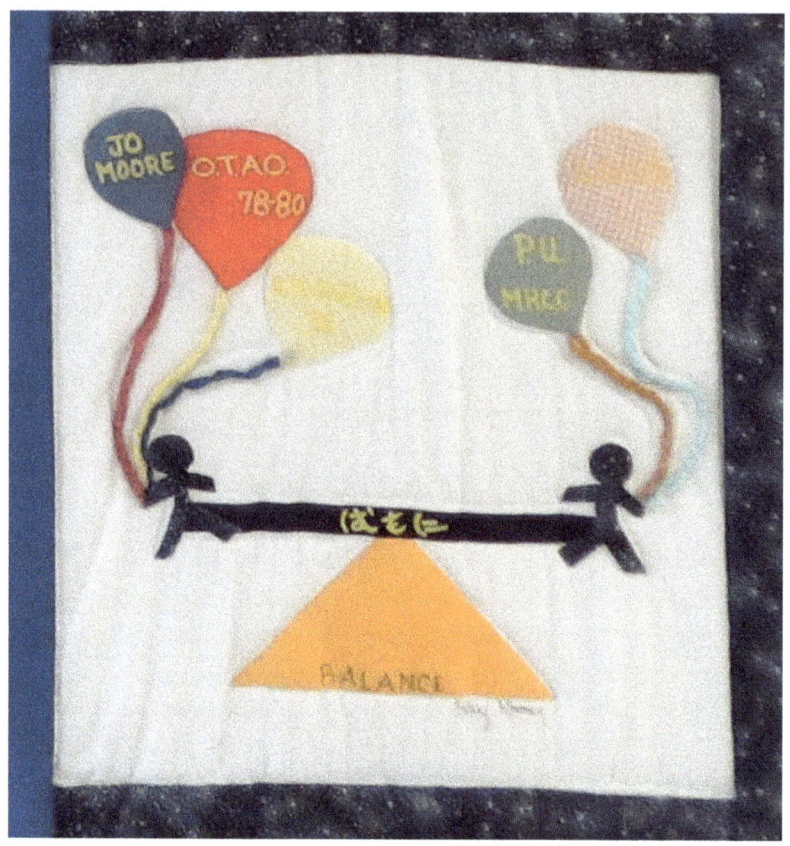

Kay Rhoney:

Kay graduated from Virginia Commonwealth University in 1967. In OTAO Kay served as vice president in 1976-1977, and as president in 1978-1979. She also served on various committees and was on the OT Licensing Board. OT work began when she lived in Japan for 3 years and started a private school for children with disabilities. She worked in physical disabilities at OHSU, and is currently with the Lake Oswego school district. The quilt square's philosophy represents balance. Balance is a key area of OT and our personal lives.

Row 4 (Left to Right)

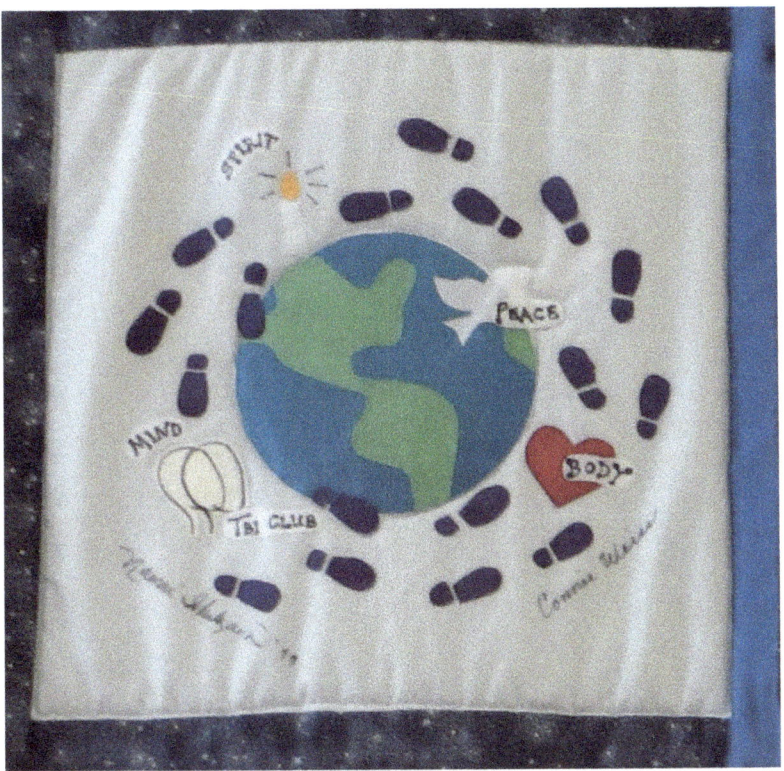

Connie Weiss:

Connie graduate from the University of Wisconsin in 1962. In OTAO Connie served as vice president in 1964 and president in 1965. She also served on many committees, membership, and continuing education. Her OT work was spent with outpatient pediatrics and in physical disabilities within the areas of pain management, orthopedics, and neurological problems. The quilt square developed when Connie went to India and found it changed her life. "The world is all linked up now" and she feels a connectedness of the world. Symbols are a heart to represent the body, a brain to represent the mind, and also the traumatic brain injury group that she is involved with, and a candle to represent spirit.

Molly McEwen:

Molly was director of the OT School at Pacific University in 2000. Molly graduated from Western Michigan University in 1973 and received her M.A. at the University of Florida in 1977. In OTAO she has always played an active role in advisory and consulting capacity. OT work has consisted of pediatrics, especially in school pediatrics, and in OT education. She worked at the University of Texas, Dallas. She was the assistant director of the OT School at Pacific University in 1986 and became school director in 1989. The quilt square consists of a maze on the square representing the "many pathways the OT leads."

Pacific University Official Seal

Elizabeth Callahan:

Elizabeth graduated from New York University in 1956. In OTAO Elizabeth served as president in 1958-1959. She was alternate delegate in 1963, and delegate to AOTA in 1962-1964. She has also served on various committees. OT work was in the area of psychiatry with some physical disability work. From 1967-1977, Elizabeth went to Korea and worked with leprosy patients, particularly those having reconstructive surgery. The quilt square shows OT schools, a rainbow for her time in Korea, the Korea national colors and the head, heart, and hand are for OT.

Row 5 (Left to Right)

Ruth Anne Moore:

Ruth Anne graduated from the University of Southern California in 1945. In OTAO she was among the organizers of OTAO. She also was present when the original constitution for OTAO was approved on June 25, 1947 and at the very first meeting on August 14, 1947, when officers were elected and some policies were approved. Ruth Anne was elected from the body to serve on the Board of Managers. She has served on various committees through the years. OT work has been in physical disabilities. She has her own business, Hand Works, making adapted clothing and devices. The quilt square is based on a design from Fritjof Capra's book Web of Life. The web spaces are filled with OT related career path themes.

Jean Vann:

Jean graduated from Washington University in St. Louis in 1950. In OTAO she served as secretary in 1951, president in 1952-1953, vice president in 1955, secretary in 1958-1959, president in 1963-1964, representative to AOTA 1965-1969, but the alternate representative went to AOTA in 1968 and 1969, and chaired Standards and Bylaws committees. From about 1963-1980, the OTAO telephone was housed at Jean's home and that was the official address of OTAO. She served on the OT Licensing Board in 1981-1989. OT work was mostly in physical disabilities with a little time in psychiatry and pediatrics. More time was spent in geriatrics. Practice setting included hospitals, nursing homes, private practice, home health, OT education at Mt. Hood Community College, and hospice. Jean is retired but is currently working as on-call OT for hospice. The quilt square depicts areas of OT where most of her time and energy was spent. The blooming flower represents the past with deep OTAO roots. The new flower bud represents the future. Mt. Hood Community College OTA Program is represented by the building (where Jean taught for 15 years). The caterpillar and butterfly are representative of hospice where she has worked for 19 years.

Kai Galyen:

Kai graduated from the OTA program at Mt. Hood Community College and laddered to OTR through AOTA Career Mobility Plan in existence at the time. She spent time at Emanuel Hospital in this program. In OTAO Kai served as treasurer in 1977-1978. She also served on various committees. Kai served on the OT Licensing Board. The quilt square shows several paths taken with steps to mark the way taken. Pins representing walking in the Shamrock Run for Dornbecker Hospital and the Alzheimer's Memory Walk. The wheelchair represents released restraints, as she wrote a chapter of reduction of restraints for a geriatrics textbook for OTA's edited by Sue Byers, COTA.

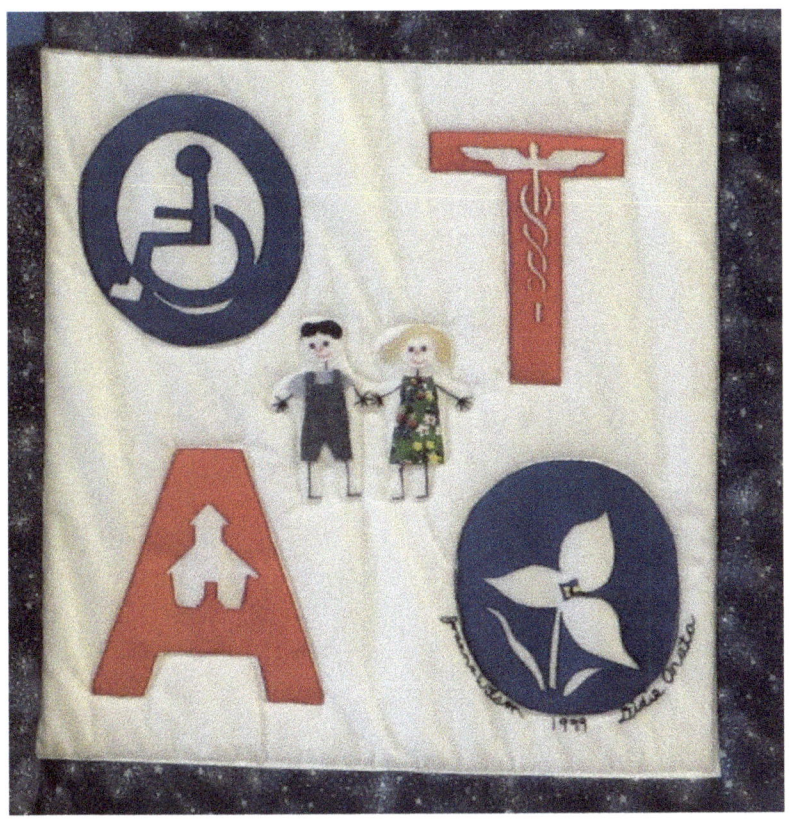

Dixie Arata:

Dixie graduated from the University of Puget Sound in 1949-1950. In OTAO Dixie was alternate representative from 1966-1969, but serving as representative in 1968 and 1969. She was elected representative and served 1970-1971. Dixie also served on various committees. OT work consisted of teaching in the pre-therapy program at OSU, in psychiatry, physical disabilities, and pediatrics. She worked for the Vancouver School District from 1963 until she retired. The quilt square focuses on children. The wheel chair focuses on accessibility.

Row 6 (Left to Right)

Norma Holliman:

Norma graduated from the University of Wisconsin in 1959. In OTAO Norma served as secretary in 1960-1961. In 1963, she was vice president. She also served on committees. Norma was the first African American OT in Oregon. OT work consisted of psychiatry, pediatrics as a school therapist, physical disabilities, and geriatrics. She worked in hospitals, nursing homes, and home health. For many years she has had her own business practicing OT in Vancouver, Washington. The quilt square represents the development of OT, celebration of the new millennium, and the Master of Occupational Therapy (MOT) program at Pacific University.

Lilian Crawford:

Lilian graduated from the University of Puget Sound in 1967. She received her Master's degree in OT at the University of Washington in 1971. In OTAO she served as president in 1986-1987. She served on the legislative and other committees, and was a liaison to the Education Committee. She is a fellow in AOTA. OT work was in the fields of pediatrics, physical disabilities, geriatrics, psychiatry, and OT education. Lilian was program director at Mt. Hood Community College in 1977-1984 when it became a two-year program. In 1985, she began at Pacific University until she retired.

Pat Evans:

Pat graduated from the University of Minnesota in 1956. In OTAO Pat served as vice president in 1961, and president in 1962. She requested the AOTA Conference to be held in Portland and it was in 1968. She al established the OTAO annual meeting and conference. As membership chair, she began the membership directory. OT work was in the fields of physical disabilities, rehabilitation, pediatrics, psychiatry, and with multiply handicapped. The quilt square is half 1968 AOTA Conference in Portland, and the other half is her school patch and jobs. The lower right hand corner is the newsletter and the directory.

Linda Johnson:

Linda graduated from the University of Iowa in 1950. In OTAO Linda served as vice president in 1967, president in 1970-1971, representative from 1972-1977. She helped establish the state's President group with AOTA. Linda is a fellow of AOTA. OT work was in the fields of pediatrics, physical disabilities, and geriatrics. She became an expert in geriatrics and even wrote a chapter about geriatric OT care in the Willard and Spackman textbook. When in OTAO, Linda organized a fundraiser of selling folding scissors to OTs at state and national conferences. The quilt square represents the folding scissors she sold. She said, "It was an awful lot of fun!"

11
To the Present

Waterfalls in the Columbia Gorge. © Martha Wegner, OTD, OTR/L, Pacific University Class of 2015. Used with permission.

Occupational therapy has maintained a strong role in mental health practice throughout the last century. Below is an article to describe our profession's impact from a local standpoint.

Occupational Therapy in Mental Health Practice

*Adapted from the School of OT newsletter

A committee composed of Genevieve deRenne, Sean Roush, Sara Pickett, Kelly Ricketts, Cat McGovern-Zloteck, Melodie Ethel-King, Kristy Fleming, Margo Traines, Torri Reichman, and Amber Black recently reviewed the rules for OT practice in mental health in Oregon. In collaboration with the licensing board the committee drafted the Occupational Therapy in Mental Health Practice rule which Sean Roush presented to the board at their meeting in August. The rule was approved by the board and has now been adopted. In addition to providing an overview of OT practice in mental health, the new rule explicitly allows OTs to assign a mental health diagnosis using the DSM with the provision that the diagnosis will be confirmed by the supervising physician. Diagnosing mental health conditions has been a grey area for OTs in Oregon due to the fact that OTs are identified as Qualified Mental Health Professionals (QMHP) in Oregon Administrative Rules and QMHPs do assign diagnosis but prior to practice rules neither granted nor denied the ability to assign a DSM diagnosis. This new rule clears the way for more OTs to enter mental health practice by clearly aligning the OT practice rules with the QMHP rules. The full rule is below:

1. Groups (collective individuals, e.g. families, workers, students or community); and Populations (collective groups of individuals living in a similar locale, e.g., city, state, or county residents, people sharing same or like concerns.)

2. Occupational therapists perform evaluations and interventions that focus on enhancing existing skills, creating opportunities, promotion wellness, remediating or restoring

skills, modifying or adapting the environment or activity, and preventing relapse.

3. Occupational therapists use a recovery model to increase the ability of individuals, groups, and populations to be engaged with daily life activities that are meaningful; lead to productive daily roles, habits, and routines; and promote living as independently as possible.

4. Services for individuals with mental illness are client-centered and may be provided to individuals in the community, hospitals, correctional institutions, homes, schools or other educational programs, workplace, or any other setting.

5. Occupational therapists ma provided behavioral and mental health preliminary "diagnosis" using standard terminology and taxonomy such as DSM or ICD, through observation of symptoms and mental health assessment, confirmed by prescribing physician and health care team.

OTAO 2004 – 2005 Membership Roster

Number of Members	Membership Type
197	Occupational Therapist
21	Occupational Therapy Assistant
46	Occupational Therapy Students
0	Occupational Therapy Assistant Students
3	Honorary Members
267	Total

The two poems listed below are from an alumni at Pacific University. As noted previously, students often contribute their creative talents to the school of OT newsletter. The below examples demonstrate how important it is for students to share their talents with the greater professional community.

Reflections from a First Year Student

This is a girl named Lori
Who cam here to tell you her story
You see her every day, and think what you may,
She's really not here for the glory

She started class searching for meaning
By listening, thinking and reading
Through mock trials and health care, her Matrix she'd share
With her cave painting she began healing

In foundations she started each day
Thinking ADL's – leisure – work – play
Add meaning and strife, and quality of life
And occupation as the OT way

In explorations she learned how to sew
She also learned how to knead dough
In leading and playing, she leaves this class saying
With groups she feels ready to go

She learned the power of observation
Through watching and home evaluation
What are people's goals, routines, habits, and roles
And would they benefit from some adaptation?

402 B was no vacation
Especially no neurorehabilitation
She learned movement and more, therapeutic rapport
And interviewing, not interrogation

People started as classmates and teachers
All nice, but she did not know features
It didn't take long to know she couldn't go wrong
With each of you Beautiful Dreamers

She's wanted to help people forever
Teaching them to never say never
Through hard work and late nights, making papers just right
Her motivation is stronger than ever

With the MOHO and Lifestyle Quiz
And all this Practice Framework biz
At nine months and a day, she is happy to say
She can almost describe what OT is

As the summer approaches she's grinning
With ideas, her head is now brimming
As the ending comes near, of her very first year
She knows this is just the beginning

-Lori Bender, MOT 1 Student
Integration Week Assignment
May 11, 2004

19 Strangers

19 Strangers, 8 days of bonding, starting to make connections...

We are the class of 2006
Starting with one boy & 18 chicks
With big hearts & strong minds,
We know you will find
A creative & talented mix

We searched for meaning each day
We learned theory & leisure/work/play
Adding meaning & strife, & quality of life
And occupation as the OT way

Certain classes were no vacation
Especially not neurorehabilitation
We learned movement & more,
Therapeutic rapport
And the art of interviewing, not interrogation

Healthcare reports were not a time for the modest
Lysse's pleather pants were definitely the hottest
Melissa danced as a flapper, looking
Really quite dapper
And Angela looked like a greek goddess

Our talents were not hidden for long
Like Jane's ability to dance to any song
Kara's jewelry-making, auction money
She's raking
With Jeannie beading, you can't go wrong

It seemed everyone knew how to knit
Katie's felt bags were always a hit
As time went on, there was music & song
And Adrienne danced like Michael to "Beat It"

Integration week we all took a chance
Remember Benson's interpretive dance?
We didn't have to wait long for Sabrina's
Beautiful song
And Kristy's artistry we all got to glance

Semester's end we all hit the wall
At Cora's we could all have a ball
Down the street we would roam,
Welcomed into her home
Where Lara's dance was the most fun of all

Practicals made us all lose face
Except when Gretchen won the
Wheelchair race
Volunteers teaching lessons,
Babies not answering questions
And range of motion in bathrooms & closet space

We learned all about Sensory Integration
With Michelle in the tunnel for modulation
Our mouths full of fingers,
A room full of swingers
And bubbles or toys at each station

Presentations gave us all a big chill
And made Lori become might ill
With the videotape on, we knew it wouldn't be long
Before Shannon would blow us away with her skill

With Emerging Practice came changes & smarts
It became harder to tear us apart
The more we all know, we've continued to grow
But Gena & Rhonda remain in our hearts

As the ending approaches there's elation
To discover our new vocation
No matter where we all go,
You'll be happy to know
That we get it Steve, it's about OCCUPATION!

As May 20th approaches we're grinning
With ideas, our heads are now brimming
As the ending comes near
Of three amazing years
We know this is just the beginning
17 practitioners, 978 days of bonding, connecting to make an OT family.

-Lori Bender

The below letter is a good example of how important it is to discuss common goals between national and state organizations in an effort to increase awareness. It is interesting to compare the below information with challenges experienced by OTAO in the beginning; membership and advocacy, for examples, are common themes embedded throughout OTAO's history. This letter is a reminder of the trials OTAO has overcome. In addition, it is helpful to consider how organizations may work together to achieve similar goals.

November 2008

Dear OTAO and AOTA members:

Occupational therapy in Oregon is entering the year 2009 with more security. How you might ask? Oregon faced an unusual challenge in November 2008. The Oregon Physical Therapy Licensing Board was looking to adopt a definition of "physical therapy intervention" that included verbiage regarding functional training in ADL's and IADL's and read a whole lot like a definition of occupational therapy.

The interesting part of this challenge was that the definition was being adopted in the rule making process, which is outside of the legislative process, and was overseen only by the Physical Therapy Licensing Board.

The Occupational Therapy Association of Oregon (OTAO) teamed up right away with the American Occupational Therapy Association (AOTA) to help deepen our understanding of the issues and definitions being brought forth by the physical therapy profession. We then collaborated with the Oregon Physical Therapy Association (OPTA) to come up with compromise language that would be acceptable by both professions to clarify that the context of physical therapy intervention in functional training is focused on "physical movement and mobility." We appreciated the Oregon Physical Therapy Association was willing to work with us and support our proposed modifications.

To make a long story short, we testified at the rules hearing and our definition modifications were rejected. We rallied to have a second reconsideration hearing. We willingly compromised further to just get the terms "related to physical movement and mobility" included in two places, and we were rejected a second time.

With a final, and third effort made between OTAO, AOTA and the OPTA, the terms were included in the definition for the final version of physical therapy intervention to include "related to physical movement and mobility" before the terms speaking of function, ADL's and IADL's, work, school, play, and leisure.

What a great relief. The future of OT in Oregon could have been dramatically altered. The future of OT in Oregon could have become weaker without a loyal OTAO member bringing this issue to our attention. The job security in Oregon could have been shaken had OTAO and AOTA not had such a strong partnership in advocacy.

The political world can move quickly and move without regard to adverse effects to any one group. In these economic times, we can get stuck in a bit of a catch 22 where cash flow might be a bit tighter which leaves membership dues seeming less of a priority and harder to pay. However, without strong membership at the state and national level, the resources would not be available to fight these types of battles, which could leave people even more threatened in the job market, and even tighter cash flow. Your continued membership in both OTAO and AOTA provides the associations with the resources we need to advocate to policymakers on your behalf.

We applaud those who choose to make association memberships a priority as your career and profession are a major priority in your daily lives. There is definitely strength in numbers and when it comes to the profession we've all chose to spend our lives in, occupational therapy, we should all continue to choose strength.

Sybil Fisher, OTR/L, CHT

President

Occupational Therapy Association of Oregon

Chuck Willmarth

Director, State Affairs and Reimbursement & Regulatory Policy

American Occupational Therapy Association

Sue Nelson commonly states, "OT is not only a profession, it is a lifestyle." Where do you see occupational therapy in your own life? The below article is a wonderful demonstration of how occupational therapy may assist in the well-being of cancer survivors.

OT Against Cancer

—Lorna MacKinnon Day, OTR/L

It's been 20 years since I received my education in Occupational Therapy. I am still profoundly grateful for that degree, and for how it has impacted my life recently through a very difficult journey with childhood cancer.

I graduated from Pacific University grounded in the idea that meaningful work, play, and self-care were necessary elements to one's health and happiness. I am keenly aware of my own deep satisfaction of getting lost in an activity like kayaking, teaching, gardening, or connecting with someone in need.

When I was accepted into the program, I did not realize how unique and fitting it would be for me. Sometimes life's pursuits and accomplishments collide with later circumstances, and give strength in unexpected ways. Though I am unable to work right now, my education has served my family and me very well.

After graduation, I spent my first 7 years as a pediatric therapist. I then took several years off to stay home with my two kids, Natalie and Samuel. My little Sam was a bit of a sparkplug, so I didn't get back to work as quickly as anticipated. In 2010, just months into finally working at a wonderful private therapy clinic in Portland, Sam was diagnosed with bone cancer. He was 9 years old, just starting third grade.

That was over 4 years ago. Today, Sam continues to fight a very difficult battle with Ewing's Sarcoma. He has lost his left leg below the knee an part of his right foot. He's endured a total of 11 surgeries and over two years of intense chemotherapy. Today, because of a cutting edge immunotherapy trial in Dallas, Texas, we have a glimmer of hope that he will be with us for many more years. A vaccine was made out of his own cancer tissue to teach his immune system to attack it. Fortunately, more promising treatments for Ewing's Sarcoma are now within reach.

Needless to say, we've had to adapt in order to live well. In fact, living well is what our family has chosen to pursue with more intensity than we ever had before.

Two years ago, a doctor at MD Anderson said to me, "The cancer will come back and there's nothing you can do about it." This was devastating news. But I don't do "nothing" very well. His comment launched me into intense lifestyle change, mostly in regards to our diet. In all my reading about overcoming cancer's prognosis through nutrition, I noticed a consistent theme; meaningful activity is part of the lifestyle needed to fight cancer. I wasn't surprised at this idea, but I was delighted to see how recognized the value of meaningful occupation is to one's health, even against such a beast as cancer. The concept isn't limited to coping with cancer; it's a tool in the fight against cancer. Meaningful activity! That was one area I felt equipped to tackle.

We've had to be creative, take risks, and make extra efforts to find meaningful activity for Sam and our family. As a youngster, Sam was fast on his feet, competitive, and highly active. He remembers the days when he was picked first for the games at recess, and still feels the apin of ultimately being picked last. He had many months of watching from the sidelines while on crutches without a leg. Football, soccer, basketball and track are no longer part of Sam's extracurricular activities. He has had to grieve through this process of letting go. We all have.

Four months after his amputation, we were with some other families at a lake near the coast. Sam got into a kayak and started racing (because everything is a competition for my 10 year old boy). He was a natural and he beat his friends! It was the first time in many months that he'd had the ability to compete in something physical. So of course, we invested in a couple of kayaks! Since that time, Sam has found the thrill of learning to snowboard, surf, skateboard, and swim. He's also discovered that he enjoys drama…of course, he's always managed to capture an audience. We've met some generous celebrities, athletes, and inspiring people who've brought unexpected joy into our lives when we most needed a good distraction. Yes, it's all happened because of cancer, but also because we make every effort to Live Well.

When Sam finds joy in an activity I often think, "This is OT!" I've witnessed him be the last one out of the water at a surfing clinic, snowboard until his legs couldn't hold him up, and swim with riveted attention alongside a Paralympic athlete. When he's engaged in that way, I know that his stress decreases, his serotonin increases, his body gets stronger, his spirit thrives and his cancer is a defeated enemy. THAT is occupational therapy!

Though it's been difficult for me to have to put my profession aside for such a long time, my education is part of my identity. I am grateful for my informed and holistic view of health and wellness. I have become a resource, and Sam has become an inspiration to many others fighting the disease.

OTAO is, and always has been, an organization dedicated to building community. In short, we are stronger together. OTAO has dedicated the past 70 years to creating a group of professionals that drive and create positive change. The below story may be thought of as symbol for professional growth. How do you see OTAO evolving in the future? What contributions can you make to ensure future success of OTAO?

The Goose Story

—Author Unknown

Next fall, when you see Geese heading South for the Winter, flying along in V formation, you might consider what science has discovered as to why they fly that way: as each bird flaps its wings, it creates an uplift for the bird immediately following. By flying in V formation the whole flock adds at least 71% greater flying range than if each bird flew on its own

People who share a common direction and sense of community can get where they are going more quickly and easily because they are traveling on the thrust of one another. When a goose falls out of formation, it suddenly feels the drag and resistance of trying to go it alone and quickly gets back into formation to take advantage of the lifting power of the bird in front. If we have as much sense as a goose, we will stay in formation with those who are headed the same way we are. When the Head Goose gets tired, it rotates back in the wing and another goose flies point. It is sensible to take turns doing demanding jobs with people or with geese flying South.

Geese honk from behind to encourage those up front to keep up their speed. What do we say when we honk from behind? Finally, and this is important, when a goose gets sick, or is wounded by gunshots and falls out of formation, two other geese fall out with that goose and follow it down to lend help and protection. They stay with the fallen goose until it is able to fly, or until it dies. Only then do they launch out on their own, or with another formation to catch up with their group. IF WE HAVE THE SENSE OF A GOOSE, WE WILL STAND BY EACH OTHER LIKE THAT.

12

Before the Future

Pacific Ocean (near Neskowin, Oregon). © Aaron R. Proctor, OTD, OTR/L, Pacific University Class of 2015. Used with permission.

Thoughts from John White

This new year will bring significant changes to the School of OT with our first OTD graduates, a search for the next program director, Advisory Board transitions, and more. The search for a new program director is progressing and well-qualified candidates will be interviewed this spring semester with the plan for her or him to assume duties on July 1, 2015. At that time I will transition into a faculty position. I look forward to continuing at Pacific to support our students through teaching and advising, and I expect to increase my research and service activities.

We also have a new Advisory Board Chair. Kelli Iranshad assumed her new role at the November, 2014 Board meeting, and brings her wealth of experiences as a Board member, alumna, and adjunct instructor to the position. We are excited to work with her and our strong Advisory Board group on a number of initiatives. An example of the Board's good work is the upcoming quarterly continuing education series (starts on February 11th). The series is co-sponsored by OTAO and the School of OT and was a collaboration by board members Sarah Larsen and Sara Marcotte (class of 2016) with OTAO representatives to develop this series.

We offer our heartfelt thanks to Sherry Hoff for her second term in the Advisory Board Chair role. Sherry was the Founding Board Chair when it was established in 2006. We wish Sherry well as she moves to Boise, Idaho and look forward to her continued interactions with the School.

Another change associated with our transitions to the OTD is that graduation has moved from May to August. On August 8, 2015, we anticipate 32 members of the Class of 2015 to return to Hillsboro after being away from campus since April 2014 for fieldwork, online courses, and their culminating Doctoral Experiential Internship. The week preceding graduation will include conference-style presentations of their capstone projects, exit sessions as part of program evaluation, a banquet to celebrate their achievements, and of course, commencement ceremonies.

In closing, one thing that we know will not change in the coming years, is the fantastic level of support from our many alumni, friends, students, faculty, staff, and practice partners that makes possible such an excellent education for our students. These partnerships also create the opportunities and foundation for the milestones and accomplishments that the School of OT community members report in the pages that follow.

—John White

OTAO Presidential Address, Adapted from the School of OT Newsletter

Greg Wintz. Used with permission.

As treasurer for OTAO from 2009 – 2014, Jan Cuciti had been active with OTAO on the backend, working closely with the office manager, being on conference committees, and learning/living the culture of our professional organization. May 3, 2014 with president Sara Pickett's permission, she was able to organize and lead our annual retreat. There, existing and including board members worked on changing our mission statement to: **"The mission of OTAO is to support our members and strengthen the occupational therapy profession through advocacy, education, and networking."** Not having a quorum, this was voted on in our August board meeting, with the members of the organization voting on this at our annual meeting at conference.

The current board has been working diligently to exemplify our mission. We have initiated pub nights, with the intent of having them every month on the same night in many locations throughout the state. We did our first April OT Month Facebook blast. We are partnering with Pacific University to do quarterly, cost-effective continuing education events. We are expanding our legislative days, as well as sending timely and pertinent email blasts out to membership. But, the biggest change that is going to impact our professional organization for years to come, is the decision of this current OTAO Board to go with an association management company to manage the backend of OTAO including finances, accounting, membership management, and to keep our website dynamic and relevant. Instead of being reliant on an individual, we are now a company dedicated to best-practice.

Jan's tenure as the 33rd president is a work in progress. Stay tuned as the Occupational Therapy Association of Oregon educates, advocates, and uses its networking abilities to meet the needs of the occupational therapy practitioners of Oregon and all of our stakeholders.

—Greg Wintz

Pacific University School of OT Future

During this transition to Pacific University at Hillsboro campus, I have added a new dimension of understanding to my knowledge of occupational therapy. "Knowledge Translation" (KT), a term coined in 2000 by the Canadian Institute for Health Research (CIHR), occurs when one moves new knowledge gained from research journals, presentations, and the classroom, to the arena of practical use, most often among the health professions: medicine, physician assistants, dental assistants, dental science, pharmaceuticals, occupational, physical, and speech therapy and public health. I witnessed KT with our third-year OT students during a class discussion where they advanced a concept learned in class to sharing its success during practical application. Through continued interprofessional and international education, research, and practice, I anticipate new opportunities to participate in and affect health care reform, now influenced from a new perspective from the Occupation Therapy Doctoral Program at Pacific University.

As I have experienced one year in the School of Occupational Therapy, I remain impressed with the broad foundation in the liberal arts that extends to his vision for contemporary Occupational Therapy and Interprofessional practice. I am impressed with the commitment of the School of OT faculty, staff, and students, as well as the entire Pacific community, to interprofessional education, research, and practice, and I look forward to being a part of the Occupational Therapy Doctorate program as we move into a bright future of health care reform.

—Gregory S. Wintz,

School of OT Director

Appendices

"Who knows only his own generation remains always a child." —George Norlin

© Daniel Tautenhan, LMT, MBA OTD Pacific University Class of 2017. Used with permission.

Appendix A: OTAO Constitution

Appendix B: Establishment of OT Departments

Appendix C: List of OTAO Presidents

Appendix D: Awards of Appreciation

Appendix E: Audrey C. Kerseg Fund Information

Appendix A

SUGGESTED COVER LETTER*

To accompany copy of Constitution

Dear Members:

The enclosed Constitution of the Occupational Therapy Association of Oregon is sent to you for careful consideration. We realize that it is long and that much of the material can be incorporated in a Book of Laws or in By Laws. However, we are presenting this material as it is because we feel that all the material is included that we may need in the governing of our proposed association.

The Constitution Committee would appreciate your consideration of this Constitution that you may be ready with constructive criticism at the next meeting of the group.

Space has been allowed on each sheet so that notation may be made by you as you read it. Remember that this Constitution must be a flexible plan whereby the Association may function efficiently both now and in the future.

As Chairman of the Committee I respectfully submit this tentative constitution for your consideration.

Grace A. Black, O.T.R.

* Copy of a cover letter sent to the membership in 1947. (Attached to a copy of the original constitution).

CONSTITUTION of the

Occupational Therapy Association of Oregon

(as prepared by the Constitution Committee – 1947)

ARTICLE I

Names and Objects

Sec. 1. The organization shall be called the Occupational Therapy Association of Oregon.

Sec. 2. The objects of the Association shall be to assist and support the American Occupational Therapy Association in its objectives:

1. "The objects of the Association shall be to promote the use of Occupational Therapy, to advance the standards of education and training in the field, to promote research, and to engage in any activities that in the future may be considered advantageous to the profession and its members". (Article I, Sec. 2 Constitution, revised 1944).

2. To promote the use of occupational therapy in the state of Oregon through education and to maintain high professional standards of work in this state.

3. To cooperate with other professional organizations in the improvements of the care of the sick and/or disabled.

4. To stimulate and assist professionally the members of the organization.

5. To assist in the educational programs of occupational therapy schools.

ARTICLE II

Members

Sec. 1. All those interested in Occupational Therapy are eligible to membership in the Occupational Therapy Association of Oregon.

Sec. 2. Members shall be divided into five (5) classes:

1. Active: those who are registered occupational therapists in good standing and who are members of the American Occupational Therapy Association.

2. Students: those in training in an accredited school of occupational therapy.

3. Associates: those persons who are interested in promotion of occupational therapy but are not eligible for active membership.

4. Sustaining: those who are eligible as active or associated members but whose interests in the objects of the association prompt them to larger contributions to its support.

5. Honorary: those who have performed distinguished service in the field of occupational therapy.

Sec. 3. The voting status of the members shall be as follows:

1. Active members and such sustaining members as are eligible for active membership may vote for and be eligible to any office of the Association.

2. Student members may not vote in the affairs of the Association but may be invited to serve as members of committees without vote.

3. Associate members shall have no vote in the election of officers

and are not eligible to any office of the Association but may be invited to serve on committee.

4. Sustaining members may serve on committees but may not vote for or be eligible to any office of the Association unless eligible to be an active member.

5. Honorary members may serve on committees but may not vote for or be eligible to any office of the Association.

Sec. 4.

1. The Secretary shall issue written invitation for membership to the candidate.

2. Application for membership may be made by any interested person to the Secretary, who shall in turn present such nomination to the Association at its next meeting.

3. The status of the candidate for membership shall be determined by vote of a majority of the membership.

4. Active members of the Occupational Therapy Association of Oregon must be active members of the American Occupational Therapy Association and pay the established fee in accordance with the ruling of that Association (Article VI, Sec. 1 of the Constitution of the American Occupational Therapy Association).

5. Members of the Occupational Therapy Association of Oregon may be requested to drop membership from the association if their professional conduct is considered a detriment to the profession or the association.

ARTICLE III

Officers

Sec. 1. The officers of the Occupational Therapy Association shall be a President, Vice-President, Secretary, Treasurer, and Delegate to the House of Delegates of the American Occupational Therapy Association, who shall be elected by the members at the first meeting of the year. These members are to serve one-year terms, except the Delegate who shall serve a three-year term. No officer can serve for more than two consecutive terms. They shall assume office at the end of the business meeting at which they were elected.

Sec. 2. The President shall preside at all meetings of the Association, shall be chairman of the Board of Management, and ex-officio a member of all committees. He shall have the power to sign all written obligations of the Association and to appoint chairmen of all committees. The Vice-President or, in his absence, the Secretary, shall discharge the duties of the President in case of his absence or during a vacancy in the office.

Sec. 3. The Treasurer, under the direction of the Board of Management, shall direct and be responsible for the collection of all dues and for keeping the accounts of the Association and for disbursing the funds. He shall report at the first meeting of the year and submit a written financial statement

Sec. 4. The Secretary, under the direction of the Board of Management, shall be responsible for all correspondence and for all written records pertaining to the business of the Association.

Sec. 5. All records and other material pertaining to the affairs of the Association which are in the custody of an officer retiring from office are to be transferred to the care of the incoming officer not later than two weeks following that meeting at which the change of office occurred.

ARTICLE IV

Board of Management

Sec. 1. The affairs of the Association shall be conducted by a Board of Management to consist of the officers and other persons elected from the membership, the number a ratio of one to twenty membership, who shall have been active members of the Association for one year previous to their election. The total number of elected members not to exceed six.

Sec. 2. The board members, other than the officers shall be elected by the membership for a one-year period. No one person shall serve more than two consecutive terms.

Sec. 3. The President shall issue orders for all meetings of the Board of Management, which shall meet at least twice a year at six month intervals, the first meeting to immediately precede the first annual meetings of the Association.

Sec. 4. At each regular Board meeting reports of the affairs of the Association shall be submitted, including financial statements by the Treasurer for interim since the last meeting, and presentation of expected expenditures for the coming interim (based on the six month periods). Financial statements shall be made at other times if requested by the Board or the membership at large.

Sec. 5. In an emergency, the President of the Association may call for a vote by mail by the Board of Management or the Association of matters that have been discussed in regular meetings or in special sessions of either of these bodies.

Sec. 6. Reports of the special committees shall be made to the Board by the Chairmen of these Committees at the regular Board meetings. Reports may be made by mail when the presence of the Chairman or a representative member of the committee cannot be present to do so in person.

Sec. 7. The Board of Management, through the Secretary, shall request the resignation of any member whose conduct has been considered incompatible with the aims of the Association.

ARTICLE V

Committees

Sec. 1. The Board of Management shall have the power to create such standing committees as they deem advisable.

Sec. 2. The President shall have the power to appoint the chairman of such a committee as the association deems advisable to meet its needs. The members of such committees are to be selected by the chairman of that committee from the association membership, determining such selection by the qualifications such members have for the needs of the committee. The number of members of the committee shall be determined by the President and the Chairman.

Sec. 3. A Nominating Committee, composed of three voting members of the association shall be appointed by the President two months preceding the first meeting of the year. This committee shall be responsible for the preparation and presentation to the membership of the ticket of candidates for election to office at the annual meeting.

Sec. 4. The ticket of candidates for election is to reach the membership at large at least two weeks before the annual meetings.

ARTICLE VI

Dues

Sec. 1. The amount of dues receivable shall be determined by the voting membership of the state association after review of the needs of the association.

Sec. 2. Any member who is in arrears for dues to the association for more than three years shall automatically...

Sec. 3. Any member in arrears for dues to the association for one year indicates their disinterest and shall be automatically dropped from the membership roll.

Sec. 4. In event of any change of status of member of the association, dues of that member are to be adjusted to the new status on the basis of six months.

1. If in the first six months of the year, a full change in dues is to be made.

2. If in the second six months of the year, one half of the difference in the dues of the old and new status is receivable or refundable.

ARTICLE VII

Meetings

Sec. 1. Meeting of the Occupational Therapy Association of Oregon shall be held not less than four and not more than ten times a year.

Sec. 2. The date, time and place of the next meeting of the association shall be determined, if possible, before the meeting is adjourned and shall be announced officially by the president of the association.

Students: Where should they go, what provision should be made for such?

Appendix B

LISTING OF WHO ESTABLISHED OCCUPATIONAL THERAPY DEPARTMENTS

CHILD DEVELOPMENT & REHAB CENTER: **Virginia Hatch**

COLUMBIA MEMORIAL HOSPITAL: **Edna Ellen Bell**

DAMMASCH STATE HOSPITAL: **Wedna Lloyd**

EDGEFIELD MANOR: **Melinda Wayne**

EMANUEL HOSPITAL: **Jean Haase Cooley**

HOLLADAY CENTER: **Jan Beelan**

HOLLADAY PARK HOSPITAL: **Jean Vann**

MORNINGSIDE HOSPITAL: **Martha Mae Lasche**

OREGON STATE HOSPITAL: **Flora Fisher Barrows**

OREGON STATE T.B. HOSPITAL: **Kitty Kemner**

PORTLAND ADVENTIST HOSPITAL: **Mary Fender**

PROVIDENCE HOSPITAL: **Linda Reed**

RIO: **Shirley Bowing**

PORTLAND VETERANS ADMINISTRATION HOSPITAL: **Mary Boyce**

SACRED HEART HOSPITAL, EUGUENE: **Sister Jean Marie**

1. VINCENT'S HOSPITAL: **Molly Paley**

STATE INDUSTRIAL ACCIDENT: **Ruth Pray Rawlins**

UNIVERSITY OF OREGON MEDICAL SCHOOL (UOHSC): **Grace Black**

VANCOUVER VETERANS:

ADMINISTRATION HOSPITAL:

VISITING NURSE ASSOCATION (VNA): **Corky Muzzy**

Appendix C

PRESIDENTS OF THE OCCUPATIONAL THERAPY ASSOCIATION OF OREGON

Mary Boyce: 1947 – 1949

Grace Black: 1950 – 1951

Jean Vann: 1952 – 1953

Louise Weidlich: 1954 – 1955

Elizabeth Irle: 1956

Robert Glass: 1957

Elizabeth Callahan: 1958 – 1959

Dorothy Richards: 1960 – 1961

Pat Evans: 1962

Jean Vann: 1963 – 1964

Connie Weiss: 1965 – 1966

Judy Rowe: 1967

Walt Ludtke: 1968 – 1969

Linda Johnson: 1970 – 1971

Bonnie Harwood: 1972 – 1973

Corky Muzzy: 1974

Grace Malpass: 1975

Susan Nelson: 1976 – 1977

Kay Rhoney: 1978 – 1979

Charlotte DeRenne: 1980 – 1981

Marta Toynbee-Bogrand: 1982 – 1983

Cathy Vorheis: 1984 – 1985

Lilian Crawford: 1986 – 1987

Candice Shorack: 1988 – 1989

NavJiwan Khalsa: 1990 – 1992

Roberta Wimmer: 1993 – 1994

Mary Jo DeVito: 1995 – 1996

Geri Aman: 1997 – 1999

Karen Foley: 2000 – 2003

Robert Love: 2004 – 2005

Sybil Fisher: 2006 – 2010

Sara Pickett: 2010 – 2014

Jan Cuciti: 2015 – Present

Appendix D

AWARDS OF APPRECIATION

In 1976, the first award of appreciation was presented at the annual conference of the Occupational Therapy Association of Oregon. The purpose of the award is to express recognition to a member of OTAO for contributions to the advancement of the occupational therapy profession in Oregon. This award continues to be given annually. In 1981 the name of the award was changed to the Grace Black Award (in honor of a charter member of OTAO who contributed enormously to the advancement of occupational therapy in Oregon.) In 1980, additional awards were instituted. They were the "Therapist of the Year" award (to express recognition of OTAO to OTR/COTA member for contributions to the advancement of the occupational therapy profession in Oregon during the past year) and the "Student of the Year" award (to express recognition of OTAO to a student member for contributions to the advancement of the occupational therapy profession in Oregon during the past year.

Occupational Therapist	Recipient Year
Jean Vann	1976
Kay Rhoney	1977
Sue Nelson	1978
Lilian Crawford	1979
Edna Ellen Bell	1980
Peggy Smith	1988

Appendix E

Audrey C. Kerseg Memorial Fellowship Fund

Image from Pacific University OT Program. Used with permission.

Audrey C. Kerseg (1910-1996) was educated as a nurse and developed a keen interest in occupational therapy while working at the Murdale Sanitarium for tuberculosis patients in Milwaukee, Wisconsin. When her daughter, Sue (Kerseg) Nelson chose occupational therapy as a career, Mrs. Kerseg continued to be very interested in health care services and followed many developments in the field, witnessing continual changes and trends in medical practices.

The Audrey C. Kerseg Memorial Fellowship Fund is the only endowed fund at Pacific University that supports occupational therapy students. Thanks to their dedicated support and the donations of many alumni and friends of the School of OT, the fund has grown to be more than $40,000. Since the first fellowship grant was made in 2009, a dozen School of OT students have received a total of #12,000 in Fellowships to support international travel, research, and program development that have touched OT clients in Nicaragua, China, South Africa, Bangladesh, and the UK. You may donate online under the Pacific University School of Occupational Therapy webpage. Either way you choose to support the school, you can know that you are contributing to the development of excellence in education for future generations of OT practitioners. Thank you!

"The business of life is the acquisition of memories."
—*Downton Abbey,* Mr. Carson, Episode 4.4

© Martha Wegner, OTD, OTR/L, Pacific University Class of 2015. Used with permission.

Biographies of Oregon Occupational Therapists

The following biographies are presented to honor specific occupational therapists who have greatly influenced OTAO, both past and future. Occupational therapy in Oregon has been forever changed by the personal and professional efforts of these valuable therapists.

DIXIE L. ARATA*

Dixie received a secretarial certificate from Capital Business College at Salem, Oregon in 1943. With this certification, she worked a variety of stenographic and secretarial positions prior to, during, and subsequent to receiving a B.A. degree in occupational therapy at the University of Puget Sound in 1949. In 1950, she had completed her clinical rotations and received her certificate in occupational therapy.

From 1951 to 1971, Dixie worked in a variety of facilities in California, Washington, and Oregon. In 1958-59, she worked as an instructor in Pre-Occupational and Pre-Physical Therapy at Oregon State University in Corvallis. In 1960-61, she was Director of the Occupational Therapy Department at Morningside Hospital. Dixie has been employed with Vancouver School District since 1963. In 1976, she received an M.S. in Education from Portland State

University. In 1979-80, Dixie worked with a training project for professionals to work with severely and profoundly handicapped.

She has been a member of the American Occupational Therapy Association since 1961. Dixie has been a delegate to AOTA Delegate Assembly, and Chairperson of the National Nominating Committee. She has also been a member of the Occupational Therapy Association of Oregon, serving as Treasurer, and Public Relations Chairperson. She also served as Co-Chairperson at the Western International Physical Therapy and Occupational Therapy Conference. Presently, Dixie is Specialist Educator Trustee on Vancouver Education Association Board of Directors. In 1977-79, she was Delegate to State Representative Assembly, Washington Education Association.

LAURA BEELER*

Laura graduated in 1989 with a B.S. in Occupational Therapy. Even during the beginning of her professional career she continued to facilitate dynamic interchange of ideas and educational values by becoming editor of the *Viewpoint*, newsletter of the Occupational Therapy Association of Oregon.

Laura continues to be active in OTAO, on the state conference committees, as state librarian, and has been recognized twice by the OTAO President's Award, 1993 and 1996.

Building on these skills, Laura has designed, coordinated and edited the alumni newsletter for Pacific University Occupational Therapy school, *Reflections*, recently publishing its fifth biannual edition.

Laura exemplifies the professional who has applied her occupational therapy philosophy to her personal development. Fortunately, Pacific University School of OT has benefited from her willingness to apply endless energy to the educational process. As her family before her, (Laura is a third-generation Pacific University alum) she is a loyal spokesperson and supporter of the school, and is now an active and contributing member of the Pacific University Alumni Council.

The concern for OT education and the high regard for a continuing quality professional education program is seen in her involvement in the School of OT Admissions Committee. Laura reads and reviews all OT school applications and during the screening process, provides invaluable insights to the Admissions Committee.

EDNA ELLEN BELL*

Edna Ellen graduated from the University of Oregon with a B.A. in Music, Language, and History. In January of 1942, Ms. Bell enrolled in the St. Louis School of Occupational Therapy, then called Recreational Therapy. It was an 18 month course instructed by Gerry Lerman from Great Britain. He was a friend of and teacher to Dr. Howard Rusk, the father and head of rehabilitation in the U.S. With this background, Edna Ellen always felt a closeness to this interpretation of Rehabilitation Occupational Therapy.

Edna took her training in the occupational therapy workshop in St. Louis, which was very much like a geriatric day care center, in orthopedics at the Indiana General Hospital, and Tuberculosis training (essential at that time) at Flower Mission in Indianapolis. This was followed by a period of training at the Neurophsyciatric Research Center in Chicago, at the University of Illinois Medical Center. She then left for Baxter General Hospital in Spokane, an Army hospital. After about six months of work there, Ms. Bell was approached by the President of the University of Puget Sound concerning the starting of a course in rehabilitation. She was very hesitant, as a recent graduate with but six months experience, and initially refused the offer. But, the college president, Dr. Thompson insisted. After consulting her former teacher, Gerry Lerman, Edna Ellen jumped into the field of education. She started the course and headed the department for eight years.

At this time, she took a leave of absence and went to Washington, D.C. intending to be married. But, Edna didn't like the looks of her man in his old home town and turned him down. Shirley Bowing, her assistant at University of Puget Sound, who replaced her after she left, then started the Occupational Therapy course at the University of Washington. While in Washington, D.C., Ms. Bell took a job with the Public Relations Department of the Republican national Committee, that worked at that time for Eisenhower. After three years, she tired of office work and desired to get back into craft work so she joined the Recreational Civil Service with the Army and shipped to Alaska. In the four years she served in Alaska, she had as many as 120 craft shops under her in outlying districts of the early warning, (dew-line) command. Edna Ellen returned to the mainland when her mother became ill, and did temporary work at a Hospital in The Dalles, and at the Rehabilitation Institute of Oregon before it moved to where it is today.

Edna Ellen, at this point, ran into Victoria Strand, one of the women who went through the course at Reed College for occupational therapists and physical therapists in 1916-17. She was an expert at weaving, her father the developer of Strand looms, and was now teaching arts and skills. Edna took courses from her: jewelry, art metal, and advanced weaving.

In about 1948, Edna Ellen was secretary to the House of Delegates for American Occupational Therapy Association. She ran into some opposition because of having started one of the first schools in the Northwest. She states, "Some of the first people thought they were going to have the whole field to themselves, on the Pacific Coast, particularly the University of Southern California." One of the early occupational therapists that Ms. Bell remembers is Martha Lasche, an occupational therapist at the Coast Guard Hospital in Seattle. She was initially responsible for putting Edna onto occupational therapy.

Notable changes in occupational therapy during Ms. Bell's time include the use of the initials: ADL's. "In earlier times, occupational therapists used skills to a greater degree than they do today. Today, they know more about the sensory areas and reality orientation – we did it all the time – no fancy name, we just believed in purposeful activity."

Edna was the recipient of the OTAO Award of Appreciation in 1980.

Edna Ellen is most remembered by her white enamel pipe.

Some of the information for Edna Ellen was contributed by Ms. Patricia A. Wollner, a niece from Gearhart, who grew up with Edna Ellen. She said their families spent every summer at the beach in Gearhart, and she now lives in the house that was Edna Ellen's.

MARY BOYCE*

In 1944, Mary was a schoolteacher in Portland, Oregon. One of her students had taken an occupational aptitude test and became interested in occupational therapy. She asked Mary for some help in finding information about occupational therapy. While finding the information, Mary became interested in the profession. During World War II, the Surgeon General put out a call for people to train in occupational therapy. She responded and the Army sent her to Mills College in Oakland, California where she trained quickly in four or five months. The Army then sent her for clinical training and to work as repayment for her training to the Barnes' V.A. Hospital for six months. She took her psychiatric clinical training at Bushnell Hospital in Utah. She worked with mentally ill prisoners of war from Italy who spoke no English. When communicating with them, they called them by the city they came from.

At the end of the war, she set up the Occupational Therapy Department at the Portland V.A. Hospital with Julia Strode as the head OTR. In 1946, Julia married and retired from the department. Mary then became the head OTR and remained there until her retirement in 1972. The Occupational Therapy Department specialized in Physical Disabilities with recreation being an important part of the rehabilitation for the men returning from the war. The department also had a Chief Doctor, with several doctors working with him, as well as corrective therapy, physical therapy, manual arts and speech therapy.

The OTAO was formed because the occupational therapists in Portland wanted to get information from the national organization. Mary was the first president of the OTAO, a position which she held form 1947-49. She was a delegate to the National Conference for five years. There were no funds to send a delegate, so she planned her vacations for the conference times, which were held in the Fall. She visited Minneapolis, Washington D.C., New York City, Detroit, and Chicago. In 1968, she was Chairman of the National Conference held in Oregon at the Portland Hilton. She remembers being treated as a VIP for one week! There were not too many occupational therapists at that time, so everyone was on the organization committee. The major change Mary has seen in occupational therapy during her time of practice is the certified occupational therapy assistant, which she thinks is wonderful! She also sees occupational therapy as becoming more specialized. Through her church, Mary is on a committee which started Club House, located in northwest Portland. The facility has grown during the past year, recently receiving funds from the United Way! Mary says there is no end to occupational therapy for her. She is constantly taking craft classes at Portland State and at Cannon Beach, where she spends some of her time.

CLARA BRAINARD SMITHHISLER*

Clara Brainard Smithhisler graduated from the University of Southern California in 1947. Her affiliations included orthopedics, working with children, tuberculosis hospital, psychology, and physical disabilities.

Clara attended various workshops. A polio workshop in 1953, a functional bracing for the upper extremities at UCLA in 1958, and an upper extremity amputation course in 1959. She also attended a workshop in 1959 at Morrison Rehabilitation Center in San Francisco on work evaluation, this is where work evaluation began.

Her first job was in 1949 with a rhematic fever program for children in the LA County Hospital. From July 1950 to September 1951, she worked at Southern California Residential School for Cerebral Palsy children. She was a Special Education teacher and did some group occupational therapy in the classroom. Clara then moved to Oregon and started working at what was then the Rehabilitation Institute of Oregon. It was an old three story home and was the Portland Rehabilitation Center at that time. The OT department was half of the basement and half of the third floor. To get a patient from one floor to the other you had to go outside. She worked there for nine years as a staff therapist, then was in charge of the department. At that time Medicare was coming into the picture and she became a consultant for a nursing home until 1976. She worked at the tuberculosis hospital until it closed on New Years Even in 1973. From 1974 to 1978 she worked at the Workman's Compensation Center, and then worked at Woodland Park Hospital in the Pain Center until 1979. Since June of 1980 she has been working at the Veterans Administration Hospital.

Clara had an active role in the Association as Treasurer, Co-Chairperson of the continuing education committee, Chairperson of committee of practice, and the Hospitality Committee. Major changes she can identify include, the increasing number of therapists and OT's expansion into many more fields, including home health.

EVELYN BRILL*

Evelyn became interested in occupational therapy while working in the Homebound Handicap Art Program at Milwaukee State College in Wisconsin. She graduated from there with a Bachelor of Science Degree in 1945. In 1946 she graduate from Milwaukee Downer College with a certificate in occupational therapy. Evelyn did her field work experience at the Mayo General Army Hospital in Galesbury, Illinois, and Pilgrim State Hospital in Brentwood, Long Island, New York. She has had various work experiences that include: The Rehabilitation Institute of Oregon, Oregon Easter Seal Society, and presently, the Veterans Administration Medical Center in Vancouver, Washington, where she is Chief of the Occupational Therapy Department.

Evelyn was one of the original charter members of the Occupational Therapy Association of Oregon. She had been the vice president of the association at one time, but found it difficult to always be involved because she resided in Vancouver, Washington. Attendance was expected at all meetings in order to meet a quorum for voting and business requirements. Workshops were held on an annual basis on weekends to accommodate all members. Meetings were also combined with the Physical Therapy Association from Oregon as well as Washington and Canada.

Evelyn remembers when occupational therapy notes in charts were always on separate forms as part of rehabilitation medicine. She says that it has only been in recent years that therapists have been able to write directly in the chart and take full responsibility for statements and signature. She states that liability insurance was seldom considered.

When Evelyn first began practicing, sources for equipment were often very limited, along with any funds to purchase them. The occupational therapist had to be very versatile and capable of designing and creating many individual items.

Because teachers at the time were not allowed to marry, Evelyn preferred a career in occupational therapy to one of an instructor. She worked in occupational therapy right up to the very day of her child's birth and was even escorted to the hospital by a Veteran's Administration car.

SUE BYERS-CONNON

Sue's life journey introduced her to the state of Oregon and occupational therapy around the same time. In 1978 she moved to Oregon from the state of Michigan with her partner (now husband) and three children (Jere, Rhonda, and Amy). She was a student at Mt. Hood Community College from 1979-1981, receiving her Associate Degree – Occupational Therapy Assistant, and was connected and contributing to the profession immediately. Recognition for her contributions at that time included OTAO Student of the Year Award in 1981.

Initially Sue applied her professional skills as a COTA employed at St. Mary's Hospital (Walla Walla, WA.), Rehabilitation Institute of Oregon, and Visiting Nurse Association. As a part time instructor at Mt. Hood Community College she became more intrigued with the uniqueness of adult education and the challenges of preparing OTA students for a fast growing health career. So she herself returned to academic life as a student completing a Bachelor's Degree in 1990 from Evergreen State College, with a focus on Gerontology and a Master's Degree in Educational Policy Foundations Administration from PSU in 1998.

Upon completion of those educational pursuits she remained primarily in academic environments for her professional work include; Instructor OTA Program MHCC: 1984 – 2002, Instructor GED Program MHCC: 2002 – retirement (2010). Of note, Sue was acknowledged for her work by receiving the Distinguished Teaching Award from Mt. Hood Community College in 1998 and 2008.

Throughout her career, Sue remained an active member and contributor to the profession both at the local (Occupational

Therapy Association of Oregon) and national level (American Occupational Therapy Association.) Some of the highlights include:

Occupational Therapy Association of Oregon:
Award of Excellence: 1985
Alternate representative to AOTA Representative Assembly: 1996 – 1999
Chair Job Placement
Co-chair Continuing Education Committee
Co-chair Public Relations Committee (AOTA National Conference 1983)

American Occupational Therapy Association:
Roster of Honor: 1989
Award of Excellence: 1993
Service Awards: 1992, 1994 – 1997
National Commission Continued Competency in OT NBCOT: 1998-99
Member Certification Examination Development: 1999 – 2004
Accreditation Committee and On-site Evaluator: 1986 – 1992
COTA Representative, AOTA Executive Board: 1993 – 1995.

Sue could frequently be seen throughout her career presenting to academic and various occupational therapy professional groups on such topics as: The Role of the COTA in the Delivery of Occupational Therapy, Skill Workshops for the COTA, OT Treatment in Groups (group process/skills/activities), Adult Learning, Learning Styles and Application to OT Practice, & Laughter and Play.

Writing contributions have also been a part of her professional skills including publications in OT Week and Viewpoint, and OTAO Newsletter. Her major contribution has been as co-editor and co-author of OT with Elders: Strategies for the COTA, the fourth edition is scheduled for publishing in February 2018 by Elsievere/Mosby.

If you have the opportunity to meet Sue and talk to her about her occupational therapy journey, take advantage of it. She has seen and experienced many things over the past 39 years and you may still see her applying the basic principles of OT in her daily life volunteering at the food bank, knitting hats for the homeless, and facilitating activities with her Yurt Group. Perhaps you will even have an opportunity to join her when she herself is participating in an activity in one of her favorite roles (self described) as a mother, wife, grandmother, and brand new great grandmother.

Waterfall. © Genevieve deRenne. Used with permission.

GENEVIEVE DERENNE

Genevieve deRenne graduated from the University of Southern California with a bachelor's degree in OT and went on to get her master's degree in OT. She started her career working at the VA hospital in Long Beach, California. She arrived in Portland to start the OT program at the new acute care inpatient psychiatric unit at Providence St. Vincent's Hospital.

Genevieve worked for 20 years in mental health, both within

inpatient and outpatient programs before moving to a supervisory position at Providence Portland. During this time, Genevieve was active professionally on both the national and state levels. She created the mental health questions for the NBCOT certification exam for 11 years, became a director of NBCOT for nine years, vice president and then president of OTAO, and a member and chair of the Oregon OT Licensing Board for eight years. She was awarded the Grace Black Award in Oregon and the distinction of Fellow of AOTA. Her career spans 40 years. In retirement, she has returned to her roots...art.

ELLEN DOWNES

OTAO and Southern Oregon: A personal perspective

Ashland is in southern Oregon, as far south on I-5 as one can be and not be in California. Opposite end of I-5 from Portland. Still, I found myself able to be very engaged in OTAO for many years. And the rewards have been profound, both personally and professionally.

My active involvement began as part of annual conference. And I was hooked. Some conference roles work well remotely, e.g. vendor coordinator, auction coordinator, so those roles were a good fit for me. After annual conference in 2000, Karen Foley led OTAO to re-shape its structure, away from never-ending committees into shorter-term focused commitments. An "Oregon OT Alliance" was created including representatives from OTAO, the Oregon OT Licensing Board, Pacific University, and Mt. Hood Community College. The Alliance facilitated networking and dialogue to develop a vision and action plan for the future of OT in our state. In 2001, the Alliance held OT "Community Meetings" in 5 locations (Corvallis, Eugene, Medford, Portland, and Roseburg.)

My commitment was to education, both annual conferences and smaller educational spring events in various locations around Oregon. I worked with OTAO's Regional Reps to develop OTAO Community Meetings in conjunction with educational workshops in 2002 (Bend, Medford, Salem), 2003 (Ashland, Bend, Eugene), 2004 (Ashland, Portland), and 2005 (Bend, Portland, The Dalles). One goal has always been to coordinate a teleconference to offer inexpensive, high-quality education around the state – perhaps in 2017?

OTAO has offered me some incredible role models, and annual conference holds that special place where we can re-connect, with the significance growing more and more important and satisfying year after year. OTAO has offered me the opportunity for leadership, which can be challenging but is so rewarding. The people of OTAO have brought immeasurable meaningfulness to my career. I urge Oregon OTs to not only join OTAO, but to get involved, to actively engage, in this dynamic professional organization. You will not regret it!

SHIRLEY B. ELINGS

In Memoriam

Shirley B. Elings, member of OTAO, died November 11, 1990, after a long and courageous battle with the disease Lupus Erythematosis. Shirley enjoyed the full spectrum of occupational therapy having graduated from the Mount Hood Community college OTA program as well as the University of Puget Sound OTR program. She worked at the Benedictine Nursing Center for several years and most recently at the Oregon State Hospital. Her obvious organizational and leadership skills benefited all of us in her contributions to OTAO, which included serving on several committees such as the 1983 AOTA Annual Conference Committee, as well as co-chairing the Membership Committee. In addition, she served a two-year term as Secretary of the Executive Board of the association.

The following poem, entitled *Today*, was written by Shirley and included in the bulletin from her memorial service. It reflects the spirit and attitude that she projected throughout her life. Those of us who knew her thank her for showing us what is possible with the human spirit and for teaching us about the courage it takes to discover these possibilities. She will be missed but her memory will linger on and on...

Today

>Outside my window, a new day I see
>And only I can determine
>What kind of day it will be
>It can be busy and sunny, laughing and gay
>Or boring and cold, unhappy and grey
>My own state of mind is the determining key,
>For I am only the person I let myself be
>I can be thoughtful and do all I can to help,
>Or be selfish and think just of myself
>I can enjoy what I do and make it seem fun,
>Or gripe and complain and make it hard
>On someone
>I can be patient with those who may not understand,
>Or belittle and hurt them as much as I can
>But I have faith in myself
>And believe what I say,
>And I personally intend to make the best of each day

-SHIRLEY B. ELINGS

MARILYN FORSE*

Marilyn graduated from Washington University in St. Louis, Missouri in 1946. Her affiliations where in Indianapolis and the Army Hospital in Utah.

She worked in Southern California and in Seattle where she was employed at the Workman's Compensation Rehabilitation Center. There she was first introduced to the concept of a team approach. She then went to Malton Canada to work in a rehabilitation center where they had a room to simulate an actual work situation. Their techniques were much more advanced. Next she went to West

Virginia where she became a department head. Marilyn returned to Oregon in 1954 and is presently working at Holladay Park Hospital. She is also doing volunteer work in the Woman's Network, working with middle age women to provide support systems, socialization, and explore new interests. She has worked ten years as a nursing home consultant and is still doing so.

Marilyn worked on many financial and money raising committees and served as Treasurer and Secretary in the association.

She feels the training received in the 1940's are skills that COTA's are learning now. "I think COTA's are worth their weight in gold." Marilyn feels there should be a door opened in every clinic for a COTA because they have "so much to offer." "A COTA and OTR working together is a fantastic team!"

When preparing for the National Conference in 1968 there were about 20 people who worked on the committee. Each person had a "buddy" to work with. Marilyn worked on the hospitality committee and they started one year ahead of time preparing packets. They gathered nylons, seeds, and perfume and included restaurants, places to get your hair "ratted" quickly, and a map of the city. Marilyn stated that in the early days the therapists worked together to help each other.

There was a pioneer effort in the 1960's when the health department gave funding to start occupational therapy in nursing homes. The atmosphere was unpleasant and unfriendly as the nursing staff of some nursing homes felt threatened. Once a month the OT's would get together and exchange information, opinions and ideas and serve as a support group for each other. They continued to meet for six years. Marilyn has made some very good friends during her OT career from all over the country, most of which she is still in contact with.

BONNIE HARWOOD*

Bonnie graduated from the University of Puget Sound in 1955. There were four clinical affiliations required at that time. Bonnie did an affiliation in physical disabilities, psycho-social dysfunction, general medicine and tuberculosis.

Bonnie had her first job at Glendale, Maryland, in 1956 where she worked on the tuberculosis ward. Then in 1957 she worked at the Portland Rehabilitation Center with the many polio patients that existed during that time. In 1961 she began working at Hot Lake Sanitarium (a long-term care facility in La Grande, Oregon). While she was there she developed a home treatment program for polio patients through the March of Dimes. After this project, she worked in Medford as a consultant to longterm care facilities. In 1965 she began working in the Portland area and was a consultant to several longterm care facilities. At this point she was involved in starting the stroke unit at Vancouver Memorial Hospital. After that she worked for Associated Home Health in Portland and is currently employed at the Vising Nurses Association (VNA). She is the director of occupational therapy at VNA.

Bonnie was president of OTAO from 1972-1974. She was also vice president a number of times. She has been Legislative Chairman and Public Information Chairman as well as an active member of the Advisory Committee to establish the Occupational Therapy Assistant program at Mt. Hood Community College.

The major changes Bonnie has seen take place in the profession are the increased knowledge at different levels of the therapists. She feels that the OTA program curriculum closely resembles the curriculum she learned as an OTR student. She states, "There is an increase in the amount and quality of education at the various levels of occupational therapy education."

In 1955 while Bonnie was on her physical disabilities clinical at the

Goodwill in Washington D.C., she was doing home treatment services. She hailed a taxi to get from one home to another. The tab was picked up by the American Heart Association. Times have changed – students are now hailing Tri-Met!!!

VIRGINIA REBECCA HATCH

In Memoriam

Virginia was cherished by many as a friend for her cheerfulness, her zest for life, her humor and interest in many people. Her teaching career has helped many students at Hull House in Chicago, a girl's school in Pittsburg, occupational therapy students at Columbia University and affiliating students a Crippled Children's Division in Portland. For her superior work she was made a fellow in AOTA in 1972 – a very deserved honor. Her students have enjoyed her patience, but they were also aware of her demands for excellence professionally.

Within the organization where she worked, Virginia was highly respected by other staff members for her own professional excellence and ability to contribute to the goals of the group. One may be sure that many people learned of occupational therapy through her demonstration and abilities. Her accurate analysis of the patient's status and sound program of therapy has done much for many children in Oregon.

Although Virginia appeared happy and colorfully dressed, she came to Portland from Carville, Louisiana in 1951 to be close to her brother. The doctors had told her that her days were limited. Boredom within a few months brought her to the Portland Rehabilitation Center to work part time in OT. From there she went to Cripple Children's Division to head the OT department. In spite of her constant health problems, she carried on an active and fruitful career, retiring at age 65 years of age. She often said, "I'm really living on borrowed time." Few people ever knew of her medical problems which limited her normal life in many ways.

Virginia was a very generous person. She loved to be with people – many a student returned to introduce a perspective husband or babies – knowing of her love for each one. She really claimed a large family in this way.

In June, Virginia died after a long series of hospitalizations. In spite of her medical problems and failing health, she remained interested in the world about her – often helping another patient write letters or visiting with the lonesome. Although her friends are glad the she was relieved from earthly pain, her friendship was a wonderful gift to all of us.

FELICIA HOLGATE

OTAO Award of Appreciation 2007 Recipient

Sue Nelson Award Recipient from Pacific in 2014 for promotion of OT Education

There have been a lot of changes in the OT licensing in the last ten years. In 2003 when I started as Executive Director, there were about 1200 licensees. In the next year or so we will have doubled that.

Licensing and renewals:

- Went from one year to two year licensing

- Started online licensing renewals first voluntarily in 2010 and then mandatory in 2012 and 2014.

- Payments for renewals can be by credit card and a majority are (saving time)

- Asked for verification from every state rather than for last 5 years

- Law/ethics exam is part of application process, is online with immediate results to licensee Board

Increase in license numbers and complaints:

- Continue to increase license numbers.

- Started with only one or two complaints/applicant issues and now have over 12 a year

- Contract with former Board member as consultant on board investigations

- Educate licensees on changes in law for mandatory reporting of arrests/convictions

- Started the mandatory legislative requirement for Pain Management CE and continue to track them

- Did a complete check of LEDS (Law Enforcement Data Base) on ALL licensees in 2013

- Fees increased in 2006 for renewals and then reduced since 2010 till now. We can keep low fee because of increase in licenses numbers and resolution of discipline cases by consent order so there are low legal costs. However, this might not be able to continue as there is more work.

- Kept FTE staff at .25 but need to increase staff hours due to increase in license numbers – in 2015 asking for .75 staff

Using electronic means to improve services – quicker and easier and less costly

- Confirmed use of emails for licensing requests, status, applicants, newsletters, etc.

- Posted all Board public minutes, newsletters, rules and information on state web site

- Confirmed every Supervision form by email for all OT Assistants working in Oregon

- Send supervision documents including AOTA, and Board Q and A to OTAs and OT Supervisors

- During renewals, supervision status can be confirmed online without paper copy being mailed

- Confirm every application received and email applicant what is still required

- Email back to every new licensee who is issued a license with information

- Option to do CE audits by scan and email or fax rather than mail

Worked with Pacific and LBCC, OTAO, and NBCOT

- Present to OT and OTA students about board, legislation, discipline and licensing

- Worked with schools to develop OT Day at the legislature

- Keep in close contact with OTAO and work with them to improve professionalism

- Work with NBCOT about exam results and changes to certification

ELIZABETH IRLE*

Elizabeth (Betty) received her Bachelor of Arts degree from the University of California in 1944. After this she enrolled at the University of Southern California and received her certificate in occupational therapy in 1950.

After graduation she worked in Portland at the Veterans Administration Hospital. Next, she worked at the Veterans Administration Hospital in Vancouver. She became Chief of Occupational Therapy at that facility and remained in that position until her retirement in May of 1979.

Betty was President of the Occupational Therapy Association of Oregon in 1956. She also served as Delegate to the national association in 1962 and 1963.

The major change that she has seen in the profession over the years has been the increase in the number of therapists. When she first began to practice occupational therapy in Oregon, there were about twelve therapists in the area. Along with this increase in therapists has come the increase in the number of facilities that have occupational therapy departments.

WALT LUDTKE*

Walt attended the University of Puget Sound and graduated in 1956 with a Bachelor of Science Degree in Occupational Therapy.

From 1956 to 1959, he worked at the American Lake Veterans Hospital in Washington and the University of Washington Hospital, where he taught in the Occupational Therapy program. He taught psychiatry. When he started the Occupational Therapy program there, he had only one student! In 1968, he also taught psychiatry at the University of Puget Sound.

In 1967, he started the Certified Occupational Therapy Assistant program at Mt. Hood Community College. This was the second health-related program at Mt. Hood Community College, with a one-year practical nursing program preceding it. He also established the medical terminology class along with the occupational therapy curriculum. The first classes were taught in an old abandoned tire shop in Gresham. The college was in a great state of change, classes were taught in trailers and were always being re-assigned to different rooms. At one time, Walt lost track of the library and when he finally located it, he was informed that faculty members could not take out books because of the move. Walt has always felt that the Registered Occupational Therapists needed the caliber of assistants that the Certified Occupational Therapy Assistants had to offer.

Mr. Ludtke was president of the Washington Association in 1964 and of the Oregon Association in 1968 and 1969. He has been a member of the Oregon State Education Health Occupation Advisory Committee since 1967.

Major changes seen in occupational therapy during his time of practice include the whole field of sensory motor, home health, O.T. in the public school and private practioners.

RUTHANNE MOORE

Ruthanne qualified for the government program to train rehabilitation specialists at the end of WWII, attended University of Southern California Los Angeles. Graduating in 1946 she worked later with Grace Black in a year at the Veteran's Hospital in Portland until she resigned to raise her family. During those years she was involved in helping others to organize the Oregon Occupational Therapy Association, and when there was opportunity to assist in licensing and certification activities as a volunteer. Later, around the late 1970's, she volunteered at Emanuel Hospital, and formed her business, "The Hand Works" and supplied departments round town with leg loops, sock assists, walker bags, etc. She eventually was hired to do on call part-time at Emanuel Good Samaritan hospitals until retirement in the 1990's.

JIM NELSON

Mr. Jim Nelson, now residing in Salem, Oregon, was influential in developing the profession. He was born in Superior, Wisconsin on April 19, 1913, and grew up in Minnesota. In 1952, Mr. Nelson entered the world of occupational therapy at San Jose State University in California. Between his junior and senior years in college, he asked for a two-month clinical assignment at the California Medical Facility. This was a corrections facility in Vacaville, California.

Following his clinical experiences, Jim began working in the occupational therapy department at the Oregon State Hospital. He developed a program for the geriatric section of the institution which resulted in "success, surprise, and gratification" to the patients and staff of those wards. He remembers getting one man up out of bed and having him folding linen. In 1964, Jim Nelson became employed by the Chronic Disease Section of the Oregon State Health Division, and worked there until retirement. His role was an occupational therapy consultant to nursing and convalescent homes. He used demonstrations for staff and clients, especially in the areas of self-help. He also developed activity programs. From 1957 to present, Mr. Nelson has been an active member in the Occupational Therapy Association of Oregon. He is also a member of the American Occupational Therapy Association.

Jim collaborated with others to circulate a survey to assess the interest and need for occupational therapy in nursing homes and convalescent centers. There was a good response. A certain percentage from the survey was needed to justify starting a consultancy program for occupational therapists. Funds were available from the Sate Health Division for this project, which expanded and broadened the field of occupational therapy. Several occupational therapists enlisted in the program which has thirty-six hours of orientation and consultation. These consultants demonstrated specific services indirectly as well as directly to the client and the facility.

Meanwhile, Jim and all participating therapists were becoming more aware of the shortage of trained personnel to work in the field of occupational therapy. He formed the committee for the development of the Certified Occupational Therapy Assistant (COTA) program. Members were: Clara Smithhisler, Bonnie Harwood, Jean Vann, and himself. There was a definite need for someone to be involved in direct service to the client as much as possible. The occupational therapists appreciated their training and realized that occupational therapy was growing rapidly along with the positions and more personnel were needed to fill those positions. The COTA program, now at Mount Hood Community College, was set up from information gathered from other COTA programs around the nation. The first program began in 1967. This was a nine-month program. Later, the program was expanded to two years. Jim said it was vey gratifying for him to see the first COTA class graduate from Mount Hood Community College. It was the reward of a lot of good work.

SUE NELSON

Sue graduated from the University of Minnesota in 1956 with a bachelor of science degree in occupational therapy

Sue worked for a few months at the VA hospital in Chicago. From that point, most of her work experience has been in pediatrics. In Grand Rapids, Michigan, she worked with the tail end of a polio epidemic and was involved in a juvenile research program. She worked for four years for the sight conservation. Her work involved starting a pre-school for blind children and a residential summer camp experience with twelve blind children.

She moved to Portland in 1958. At the original site of RIO, she had a vocational grant to test pre-vocational skills with cerebral palsy patients. After that, she worked in the Vancouver Public School System.

In 1960, she got married, had children and dropped out of occupational therapy for ten years. Then in 1970, she took a reactivation course promoted by AOTA and sponsored by the state association. This was a self-study updating process to get back into the professional level of skill.

In 1971 she was in private practice as a community consultant in pediatrics. There were three contracts in her work; Beaverton School District, Clark County School District, and the Vancouver School District. She was a consultant for two years at the Beaverton School District and then was put on the regular staff.

Sue gave up private practice in 1974 to work for the Beaverton school system as a pre-school consultant and team-taught handicapped three and four year olds. Then in 1973, she worked for eight months with Down Syndrome children and began the Infant Development Program.

When she went to school, psychiatric emphasis on practice, was Fruedian. The whole thrust now is far from the basic academic preparation. Because of the rapid growth in the theory base of the profession, a tremendous stress on therapists to be updated in the field exists. She can tell the age of the therapist when she says something Freudian and they do or don't respond.

Sue feels that the attitude toward licensure has changed. Six years ago the attitude of the National Association was not in favor of licensure. Oregon was the eigth state to pass a licensure bill. The National Association has changed to a more positive attitude. The National Association now has a real grass roots association, that is dealing with practice and therapists on a day to day problem level. There has been a tremendous change to all our advantages. She feels very positive about the changes and states, "I think the need for occupational therapists will increase." Sue was the recipient of the OTAO Award of Appreciation in 1978.

KAY RHONEY*

Kay attended Virginia Commonwealth University in Richmond, Virginia, where she received her degree in 1967. From 1968-70 she worked at Chapel Hill North Carolina in physical disabilities. She then traveled to Japan and took a part time job working with handicapped children. When she moved to Oregon in 1973, she became employed at the University of Oregon Health Sciences Center. She remained there as Director of Occupational Therapy until 1979 when she retired from practice upon the birth of her daughter.

Kay has been an active participant in OTAO since she moved to this state. She was president of the association in 1978 and 1979. She has also served as vice president, chairman of continuing education, and a member of the public relations committee. She believes that you "miss a lot" when you are not involved and that you get as much out of the association as you give.

The major changes in occupational therapy that Kay has seen include the vast growth of the profession, the variety of occupational therapy programs, and the variety of people with different ideas. She feels that Oregon is unique with our well organized an supportive association with members who are sharing ideas and information.

Kay was the recipient of the Award of Appreciation in 1977.

AARON R. PROCTOR

Aaron's journey to finding the career of occupational therapy was actually by accident. After moving to Portland in 2005 from northern Utah, he was employed by a financial insurance company while attending evening classes at Portland State University. He earned a Bachelor of Arts in English in 2009.

After college, Aaron began exploring other career options. He was interested in health care management and nursing so he decided to volunteer one afternoon per week at Legacy Good Samaritan Hospital in the Cardiac Rehab Unit. After a couple of weeks, he was introduced to an occupational therapist at the Rehabilitation Institute of Oregon. He was instantly intrigued to learn more.

He enrolled at Pacific University School of Occupational Therapy in 2012. He reflects fondly on his time in graduate school as he was introduced to new friends and colleagues. Learning about occupational therapy history, theory, application, and research continues to inspire both his personal and professional life.

He earned one of the OTAO student scholarships in 2013, the AOTF student scholarship in 2014, and the Diversity Development and Community Service Award from Pacific University upon graduation in 2015. Many of his colleagues and friends will remember his farewell address at the graduation ceremony in which he hula hooped to one of his favorite songs in an effort to teach others you are never too old to learn something new. He graduated with a doctorate degree in occupational therapy and is very proud to be a part of this venture. He is eager to begin research in order to contribute to the profession's growth.

Aaron currently practices occupational therapy in an acute care setting. He often thinks of his occupational therapy predecessors and is inspired by their rich history. For without their efforts, our profession would be limited.

Aaron began working on Sue Nelson's book as a graduate student work-study project in 2014. At the time, he did not understand how contributions of OTAO members helped to support our profession at national and state levels. This work has given Aaron a newly found appreciation for how occupational therapy has developed. A long term goal of his is to use this text to inform new occupational therapy students about many important OTAO endeavors in order to support the organization's membership and evolution.

DOTTIE RICHARDS

Dottie graduated from the University of Oregon in 1943 with a B.S. in Physical Education. It was at the time of the war when she got into the Federal Government Service. She worked in the clinical capacity with various agencies for 16 years (at the coast, for the Bureau of Land Management, the Forest Service, and the Maritime Commission.) At that time, she had a friend who was an occupational therapist, Betty Irle. One night, when they were just having a social evening, Betty showed Dottie how to make a leather belt which Dottie enjoyed so much that she made the comment, "You'd make a good OT." One thing led to another and Dottie began to get curious about it. It wasn't many weeks before Dottie enrolled in the occupational therapy program at the University of Puget Sound. She took the certificate course since she already had her degree. She graduated from there in 1956 and was the first student to take all her affiliations in the Portland area. They had just opened up the pediatric affiliation at the Crippled Children's Division and she was Virginia Hatch's first student. Her psychiatric affiliation was at the Morningside Hospital, which was out where Mall 205 is now. That is where all the mental patients from Alaska were brought. It was a large facility with acres of ground which had a farm and cannery. There was also a shoe shop and some of the OT's had lots of work to do that we call today, industrial therapy. Dottie also did a tuberculosis affiliation at the T.B. Hospital under grace Black, one of the pioneers in OT in Oregon. She did her physical disabilities training at RIO.

Dottie's first job was at Holladay Park Hospital working with Jean Vann at the time when they were finishing up the polio epidemic. She was there for a year on her own after Jean Vann left. Elizabeth Callahan replaced Dottie when she left to got the V.A. Hospital to work with the friend who introduced her to OT. She worked there for five years.

For a while, Dottie quit the profession and went to the Chapel of the Hills to be a full time Youth Director and started studies at the Multnomah School of the Bible. After on year, she realized she really liked it and took the three year degree course which took her five years to get. She worked at the college in public relations, which was the most exciting and challenging job she ever had. She learned a tremendous amount on that job and it has applied to many OT related things. She was offered a job at Dammasch State Hospital in 1967 and worked under Mary Tender for four years at $600.00 per month. She became the department head in 1971.

Dottie has been very active in the OTAO. The first year, she worked on the convention in Oregon which included Oregon, Washington, and British Columbia. Her responsibilities included Treasurer of the OT Association, President for two years, serving on the membership committee, editor of the newsletter, and liaison for State of Oregon Association and the National Association. The major change Dottie has seen here in her practicing years are the third party payments and licensure bill.

JUDY ROWE*

Judy received a bachelor of science degree in occupational therapy, with honors, from the University of Puget Sound in 1962. This same year she married Ron Rowe. They had two children.

Before she came to Oregon, she worked as a staff therapist at the H.T. Buckner Rehabilitation Center. In 1965 she became co-director of occupational therapy at the University of Oregon Medical School. She was consultant in the establishment of the stroke unit at Good Samartian Hospital in 1969. From 1966-1971 she was a consultant and had a private practice in occupational therapy. She has been employed since 1971 at the Holladay Center for Physically Handicapped Children of Portland, Oregon, Public School District. While at the Holladay Center she has been the Department Chairman and Director of Clinical Affiliates.

At the first meeting of OTAO that she attended she was elected secretary. She states, "Talk about getting new people into a job fast. There were only about 10-15 people at the meeting, and that was usual. Of course everyone had a job of some kind. I did not realize, however, that along with the job of secretary came the job of newsletter editor." Judy noted that Connie Weiss, Virginia Hatch, and Steve Moreland came to her rescue and typed the newsletter each month. In 1966 she was elected president and served for two years. Judy states, "During that time I inherited the task of planning a conference for OT's and PT's in Oregon, Washington, and British Columbia, entitled Western International Conference. It was held at the Benson Hotel and I think 150 therapists attended.

Medicare was beginning to be discussed and it seems like there was at least one meeting a week of some board or another discussing implementation."

The 1968 AOTA conference was held in Portland. Judy, Marilyn Forse, and Lois Walsh were on the hospitality committee. They worked at the hospitality desk along with practically everyone in the association. Judy says that it was time when many people served on more than one committee.

In 1972 Judy became the Alternate Delegate to the national association from Oregon. She remained in that position until the spring of 1978 when she became the Representative Delegate.

JEAN VANN*

Jean graduated from high school in St. Louis, Missouri. She moved to St. Louis with her parents from Portland, Oregon. After high school she attended Washington University. Her first clinical affiliation was in pediatrics at St. Louis City Hospital. Abandoned children made up half of the patient population. The children were then adopted or placed in foster homes. Other affiliations were at the Eastern State Hospital in Williamsburg, Virginia working in psycho-social dysfunction; Minneapolis Curative Workshop working with out-patients: orthopedics, and cerebral palsy nursery; and at Jefferson Barracks Veteran's Hospital in St. Louis, Missouri working with physical dysfunction and general medicine.

After completing her training in occupational therapy, Jean moved back to Portland, Oregon, in June 1950. Her first job was at Holladay Park Hospital from 1950-57. The occupational therapy department work area consisted of a linen closet when she started. She worked primarily with polio and psychiatric patients. Jean's next job was at Morningside Hospital, a psychiatric hospital for Native Alaskans. The hospital was located where Mall 205 now stands. The patients Jean worked with did scrimshaw, painting, sculptures, upholstery, and shoemaking. They also had industrial therapy, a farm and a dairy. Occupational therapy took over the cannery when the cannery men quit. Other jobs that Jean has had include: Holladay Center School for Children, part time at the Rehabilitation Center (now called RIO) and the University Health Science Center. She was also on call at Emanuel Hospital. In 1957 she went into private practice part-time. She contracted with the March of Dimes, Arthritis Foundation, Muscular Dystrophy, Good Samaritan Hospital, Hillsboro Hospital and Crippled Children's Division. She has also been affiliated with home health (since it began.) Jean is now teaching at Mt. Hood Community College in the Occupational Therapy Assistant program.

In 1951, Jean was secretary of the Occupational Therapy Association of Oregon. She has also served two terms as President (total of four years.) In addition, she has been on the bylaws committee, standards committee, delegate, and now has the Occupational Therapy Association of Oregon telephone and address for information and referrals to members. She was the recipient of the first Award of Appreciation in 1976.

The major change in occupational therapy that Jean has seen, has been the growth of the profession. When Jean came to Oregon in 1952 there were only about 17 to 20 occupational therapists. She states, "Occupational therapy has come a long way as professionalism goes, especially in the past five years. Redefining the roles and definition of occupational therapy has created major changes, also."

An amusing story Jean remembers is when working at Morningside Hospital. Pital, one of the smallest cows in the dairy, produced the most milk. When the cow went out to pasture, she dragged her udder, and it hurt her to be milked. Occuaptional therapy was called in to make a "bra" for her, which was quite effective. They had to make two; one for wash, one for wear. There was usually a cow bra hanging up to dry in the barn. Another time, when occupational therapy took over the cannery at Morningside, they used the wrong sized cans. They canned 64 gallons of raspberries in pea cans accidently, so the patients and staff had plenty of raspberries for a while.

CONNIE WEISS

Connie Weiss got into OT in her junior year at the University of Wisconsin. Her first exposer to patients was after her junior year, in her first clinical experience at the VA hospital in Madison. Connie graduated in 1962, and continued her clinical affiliations at the Langley-Porter Neuropsychiatric Institute in California for three months, the University of Oregon Medical School for three months, and Rancho Los Amigos in California.

Connie married her husband, Steve, after graduation, but before beginning her affiliations. When she finished her last affiliation in California in March 1963, Connie moved up to Oregon to join her husband in Portland. Her first job was working in the new, one-man OT Department at Emanuel Hospital for two weeks while the OT recovered from mononucleosis. She then worked at the medical school for one month while waiting for a position to pen at Crippled Children's Division (CCD).

Virginia Hatch started the two person OT Department at Crippled Children's Division. Connie worked there for four years, until her first daughter was born. The children she worked with were all out-patients. She did mostly work/play activities, some perceptual-motor, and some work with amputee children. Many of the children had Cerebral Palsy and learning disabilities. Virginia Hatch knew Bobath treatment, but didn't use it much at the time.

After working at CCD for four years, Connie took eight years off from active working to raise her two daughters. In 1969 she taught an Anatomy & Physiology class for COTA students at MHCC. During the years she wasn't working, Connie became very active and involved in OTAO and various OT groups.

Connie began working at Emanuel Hospital part time about six years ago. She has worked on the pain unit, with orthopedic patients in rehab, and now works nearly full time in the main house with a variety of patients.

While still in school, Connie was the president of the student OT association. Her involvement in OTAO began shortly after she moved to Oregon and said she would not get involved.

Connie attended her first OT meeting to meet people in the Portland area, at which time Jean Vann roped her into becoming the membership chairman. The next year Connie was vice-president, which included being program chairman, setting up meetings. The following year she was president, and worked on putting out the newsletter and lobbying with the legislature in Salem.

In 1968 the National Conference was here, and Connie was the secretary for the group organizing the conference, and spent many hours sending out letters.

In her years of involvement in OTAO, Connie has seen a lot of growth: more professionalism, more things getting done, better communication with National and other states, and more publicity. During the late 1960's OTAO started having continuing education committee, setting up standards of practice, and the Annual OTAO Conference.

Jim Nelson, who worked for the state as OT representative, got together a group of people to help get rid of architectural barriers. Connie got involved in this for a few years. This group was the start of the Oregon Architectural Barrier Association, which set up some laws to help eliminate architectural barriers from many public buildings.

Changes Connie has seen in the field of OT include more education, and more scientific approach about disease processes, and more emphasis on Neurodevelopmental Treatment (NDT). NDT was around before, but was not so well accepted.

Connie feels that OT is more visible now than it used to be. When she first came to Oregon, most of the OT departments had only one or two people. Now many bigger departments are found in many different facilities. More therapists are found in the schools now, instead of mostly in hospitals, as before.

One amusing situation Connie remembers is about a patient with claw-toes, who could not walk because of it. So, she cut out some shoes to fit his feet, the patient put them on and went for a walk. The patient took a short walk and came back, saying it wasn't any better, something just didn't feel right. So Connie had him take off his shoe, and there in the bottom of it was the shoe horn he had used to put it on.

www.ingramcontent.com/pod-product-compliance
Lightning Source LLC
Chambersburg PA
CBHW041956080526
44588CB00021B/2755